Copyright 2015

WE COLOR
ADULT COLORING BOOK - EPISODE 2

Colour therapy is a growing trend among adults, both young and old, everything from the very simple to complex designs are being put out there, and it is taking off everywhere ! It is used in many countries. This is one method that professionals are using in the treatment of many illnesses and for therapy, Anxiety, depression, chronic pain such as 'fibromyalgia' and other chronic pain sufferers, it has amazing therapeutic value, this is a great way to relieve stress and help take your mind off of everything and focus on creating, it is also being used on stroke victims to help teach hand and eye coordination, movement and recognition.

There is no right or wrong way to color, as a matter of fact there are many !
Below are a few examples of the ways i choose colors, it depends on my mindset, my pain level, the amount of time I have and of course the drawing.

- Colour Schemes
- Varying shades of one color
- Just pick a colour randomly or close my eyes and pick. (This is fun and often turns out extremely well)

You don't have to be an artist; you just need to know how to use a pen, pencil, marker or crayon. You are only limited by your imagination ! If you want a purple cow or perhaps a pink moon then by all means, go for it, the tricks will come with time and experience.

If you will notice, along the outer edges of DICEBIRD's designs, there is a border. Try shading it in very lightly with coordinating colours or however you wish and see it take on a whole new form. It's lovely left alone but it is very lovely with a touch of colour as well.

Hope you enjoy,
Athena McNeill
Supporter and friend of DICEBIRD

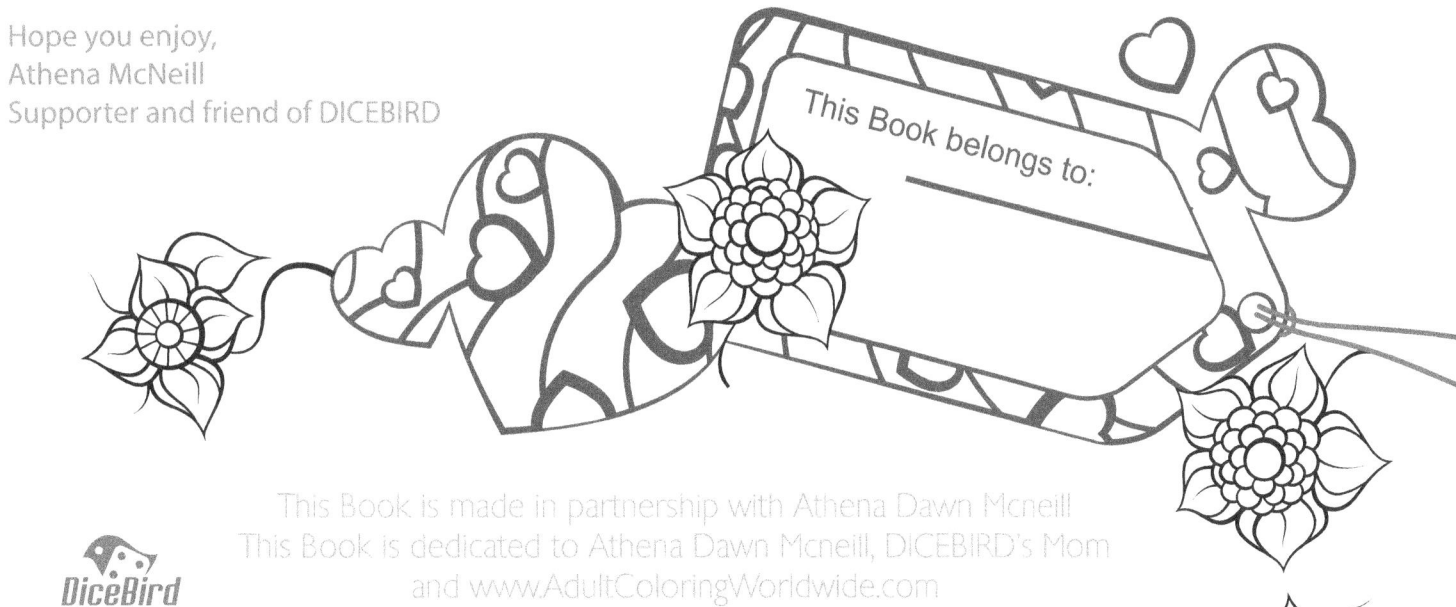

This Book belongs to:

DiceBird
www.DiceBird.com

This Book is made in partnership with Athena Dawn Mcneill
This Book is dedicated to Athena Dawn Mcneill, DiCEBIRD's Mom
and www.AdultColoringWorldwide.com

Many thanks to all of the facebook coloring community for their support

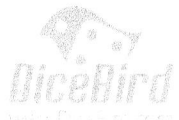

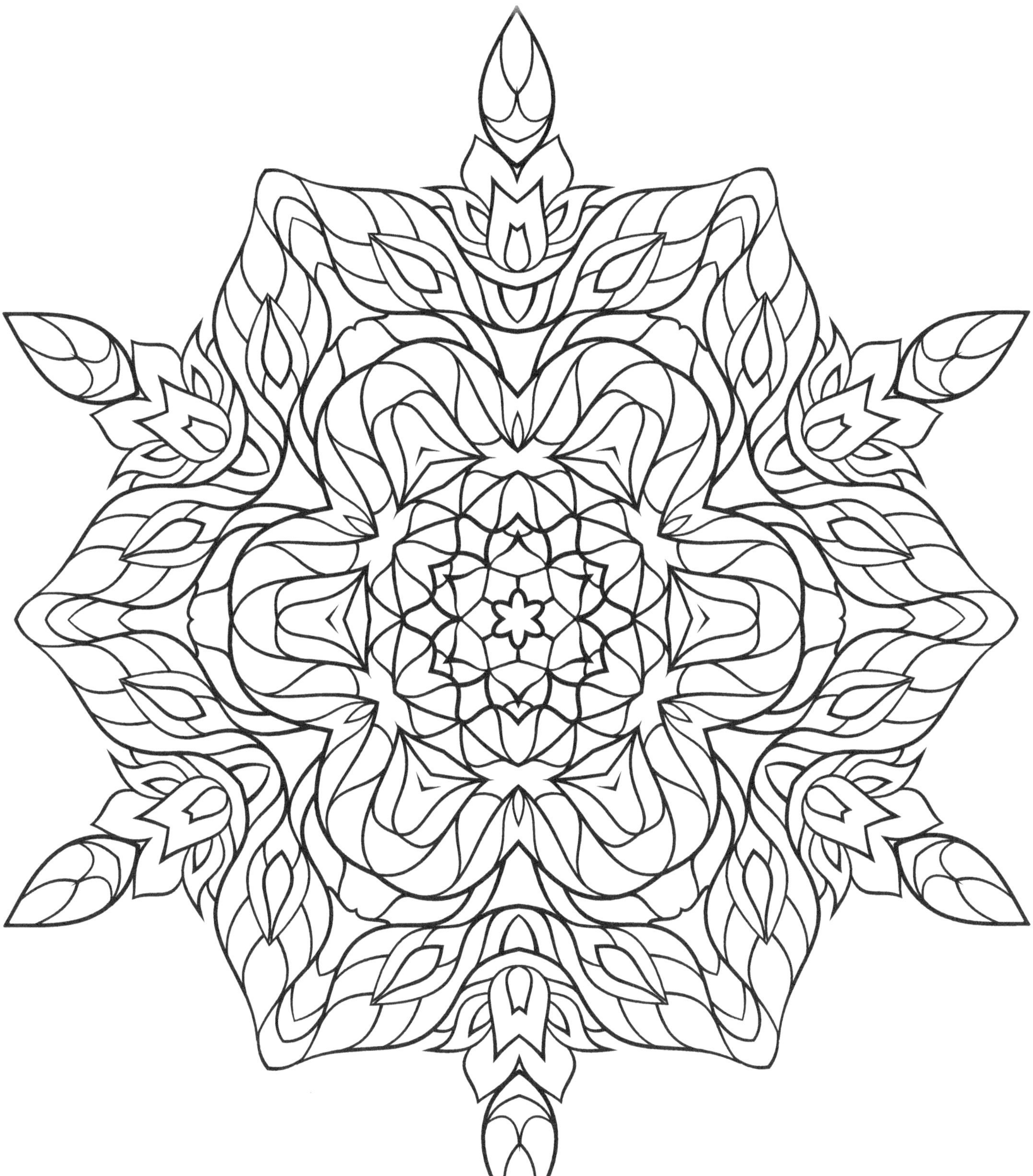

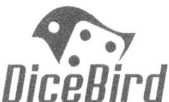

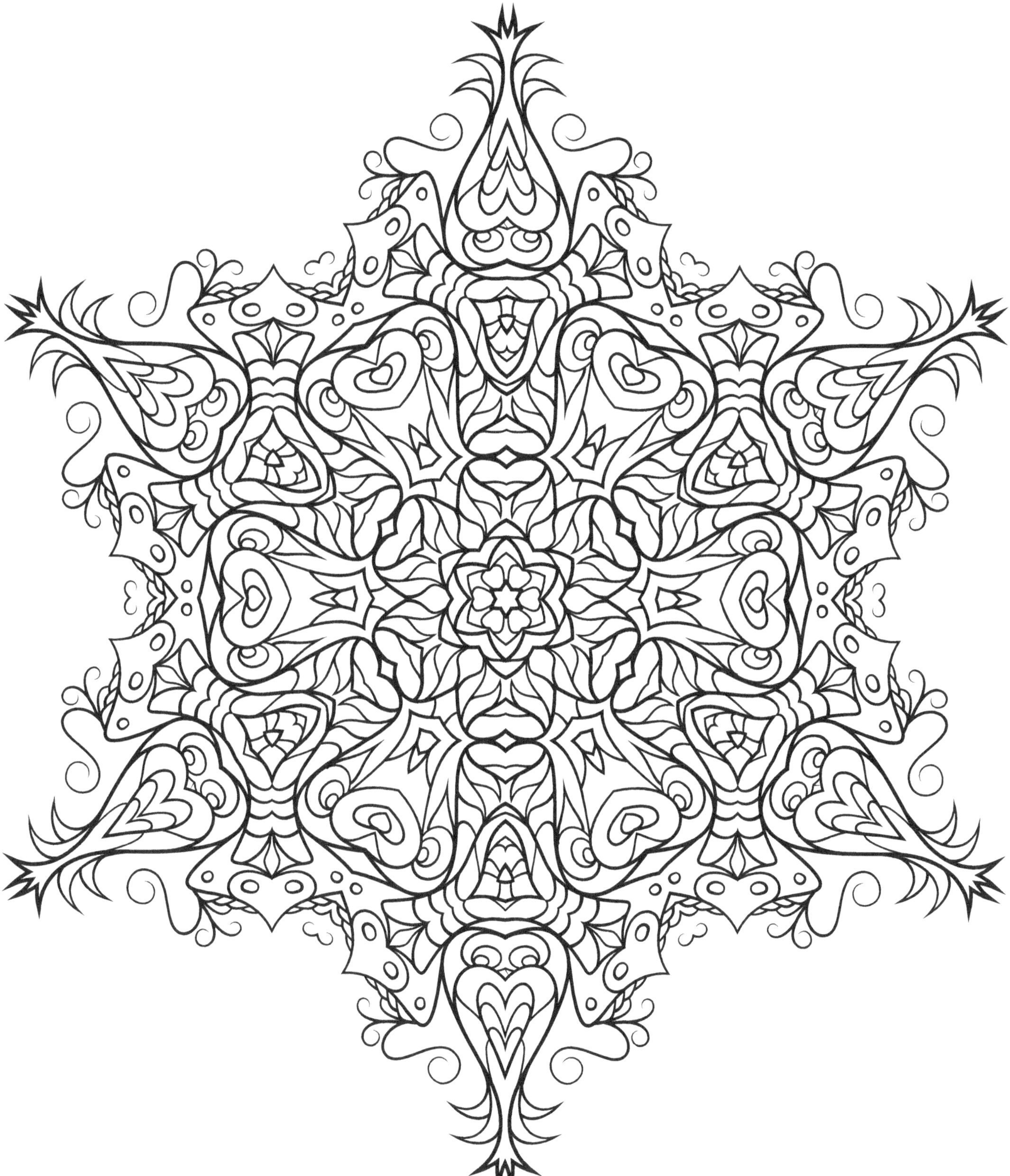

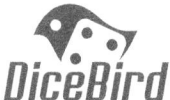

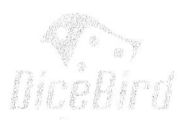

Deborah

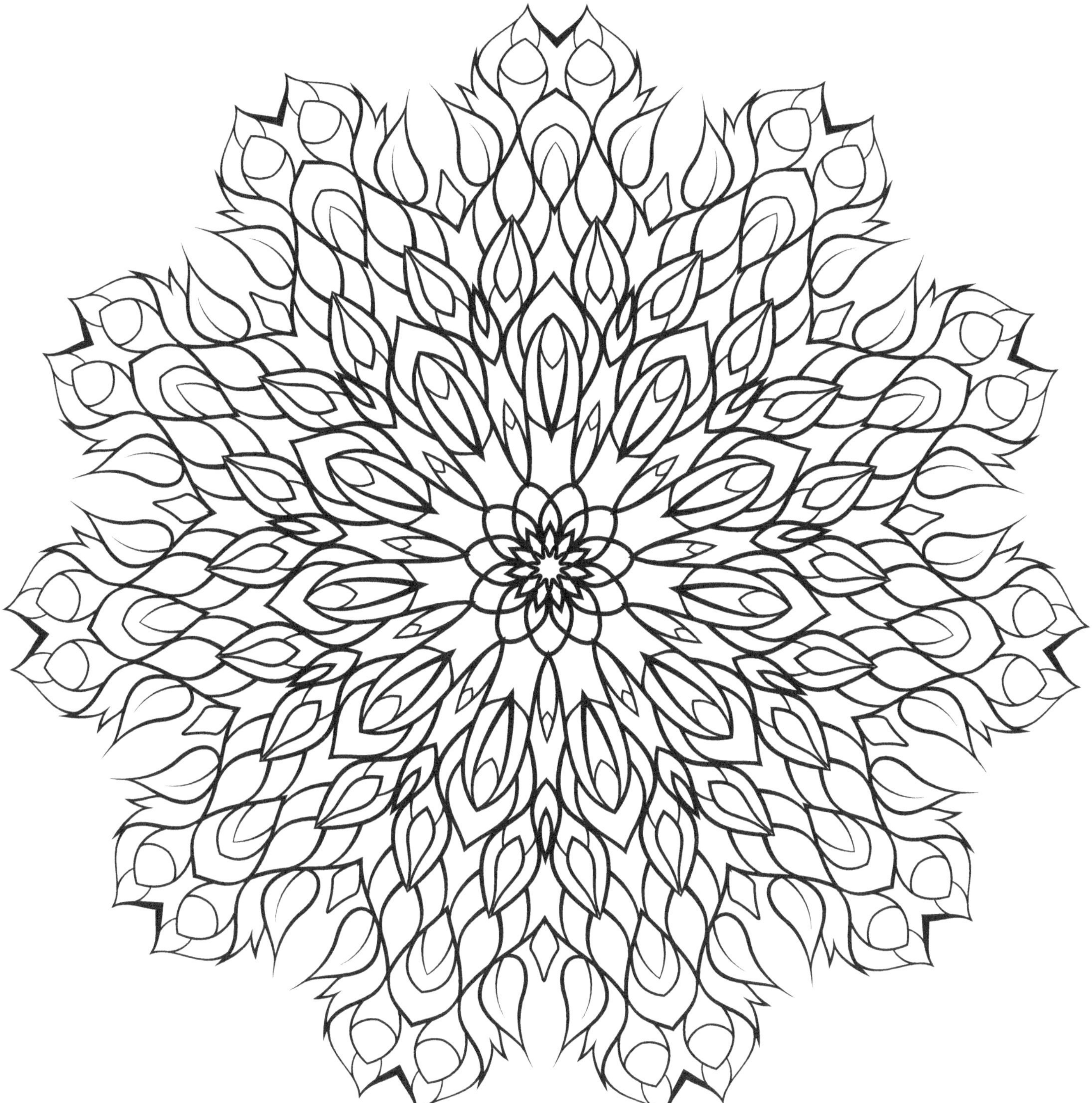

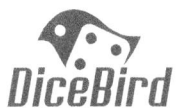

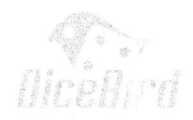

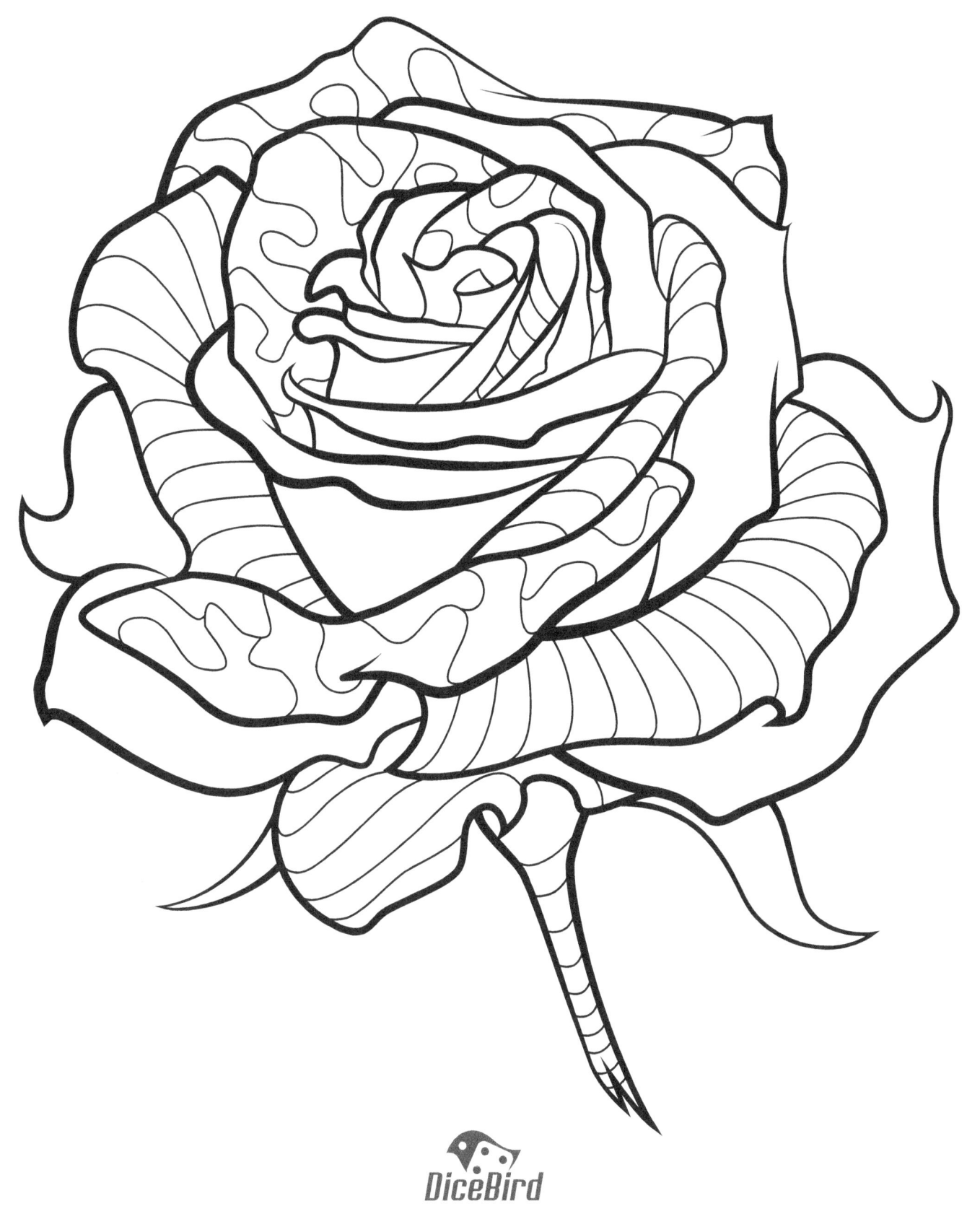

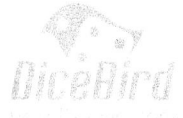

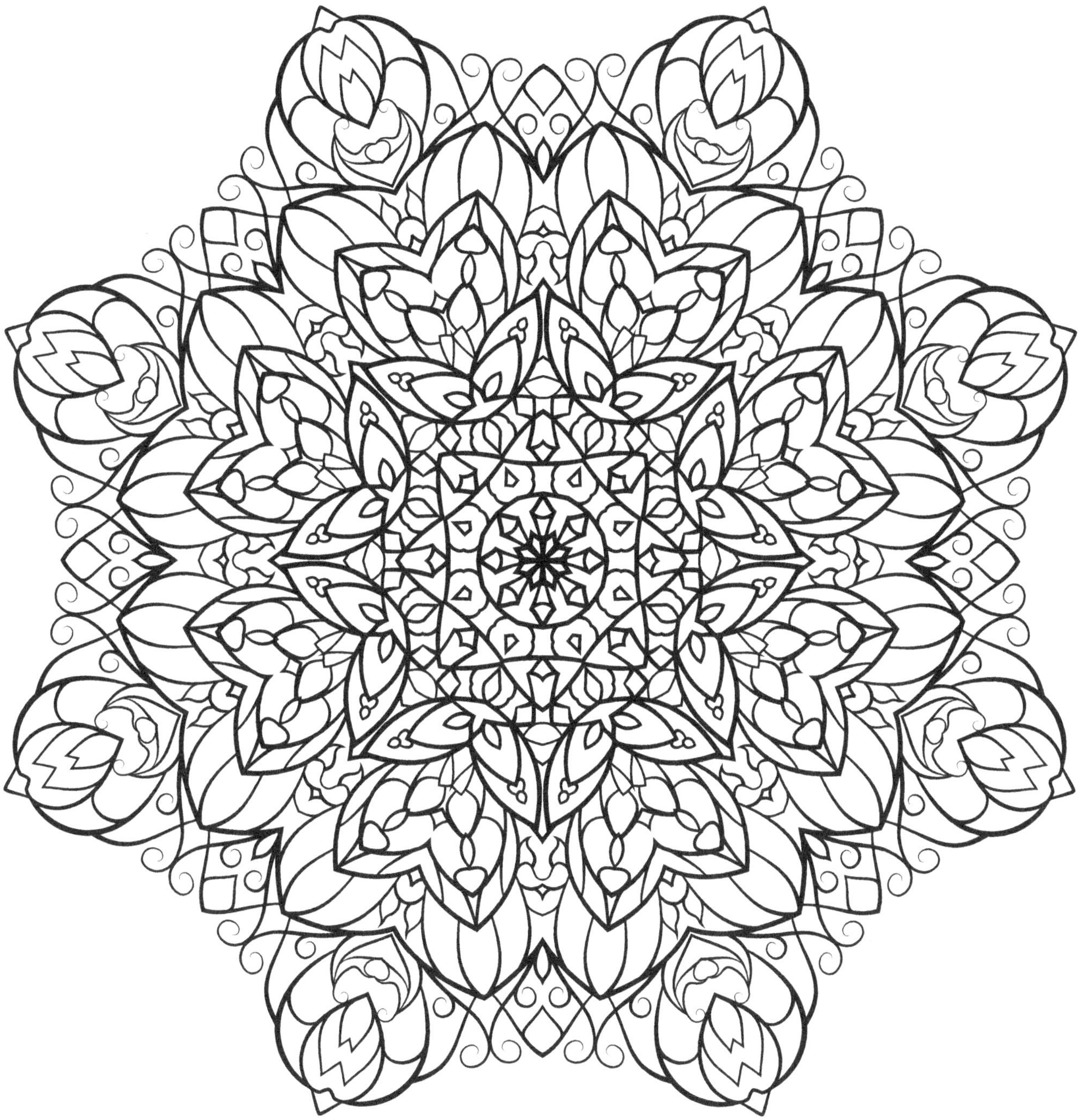

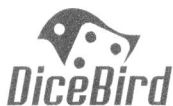

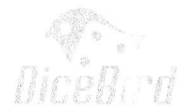

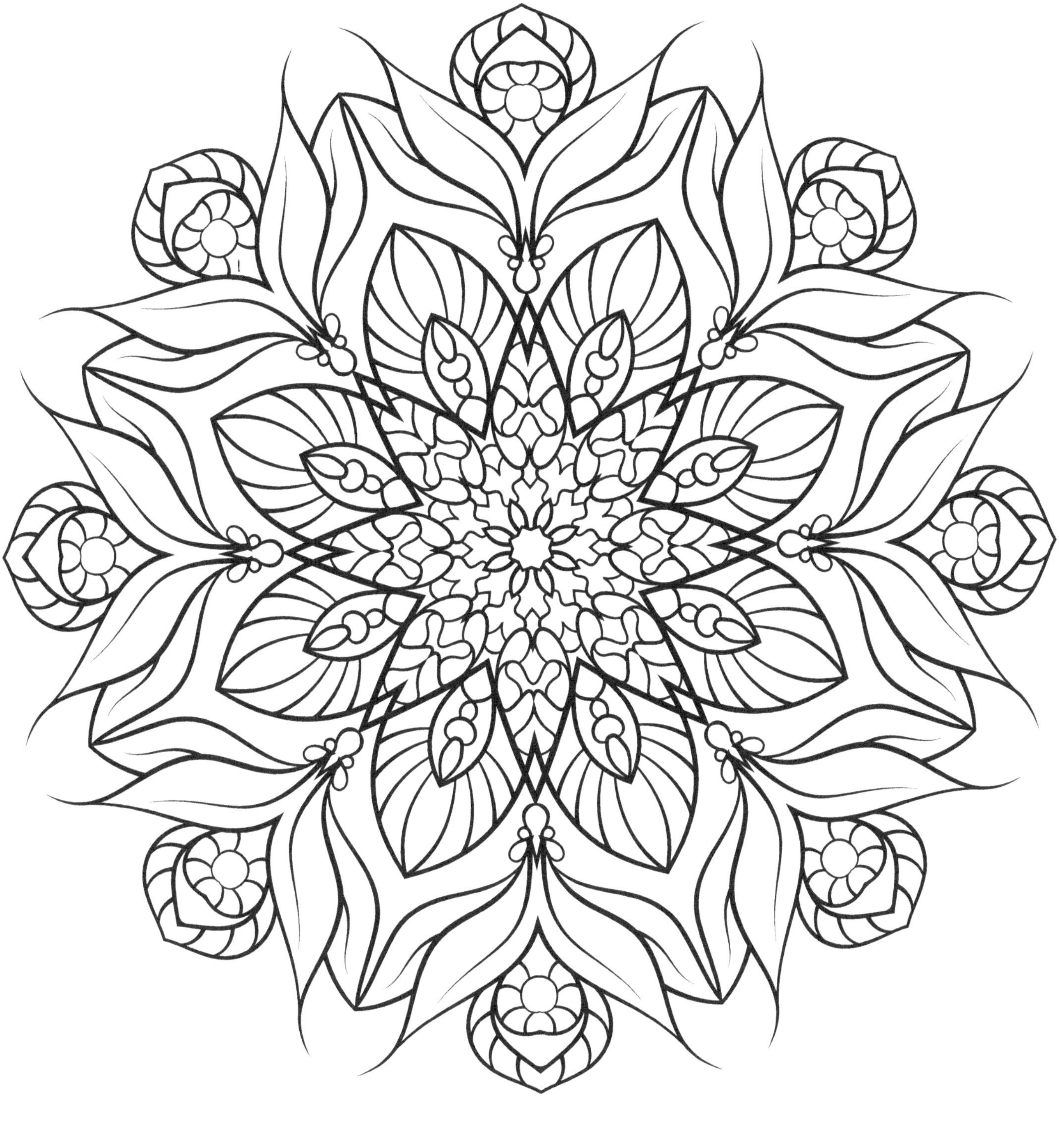

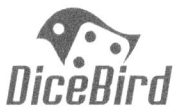

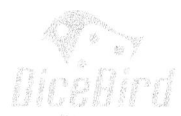

Fish Eye

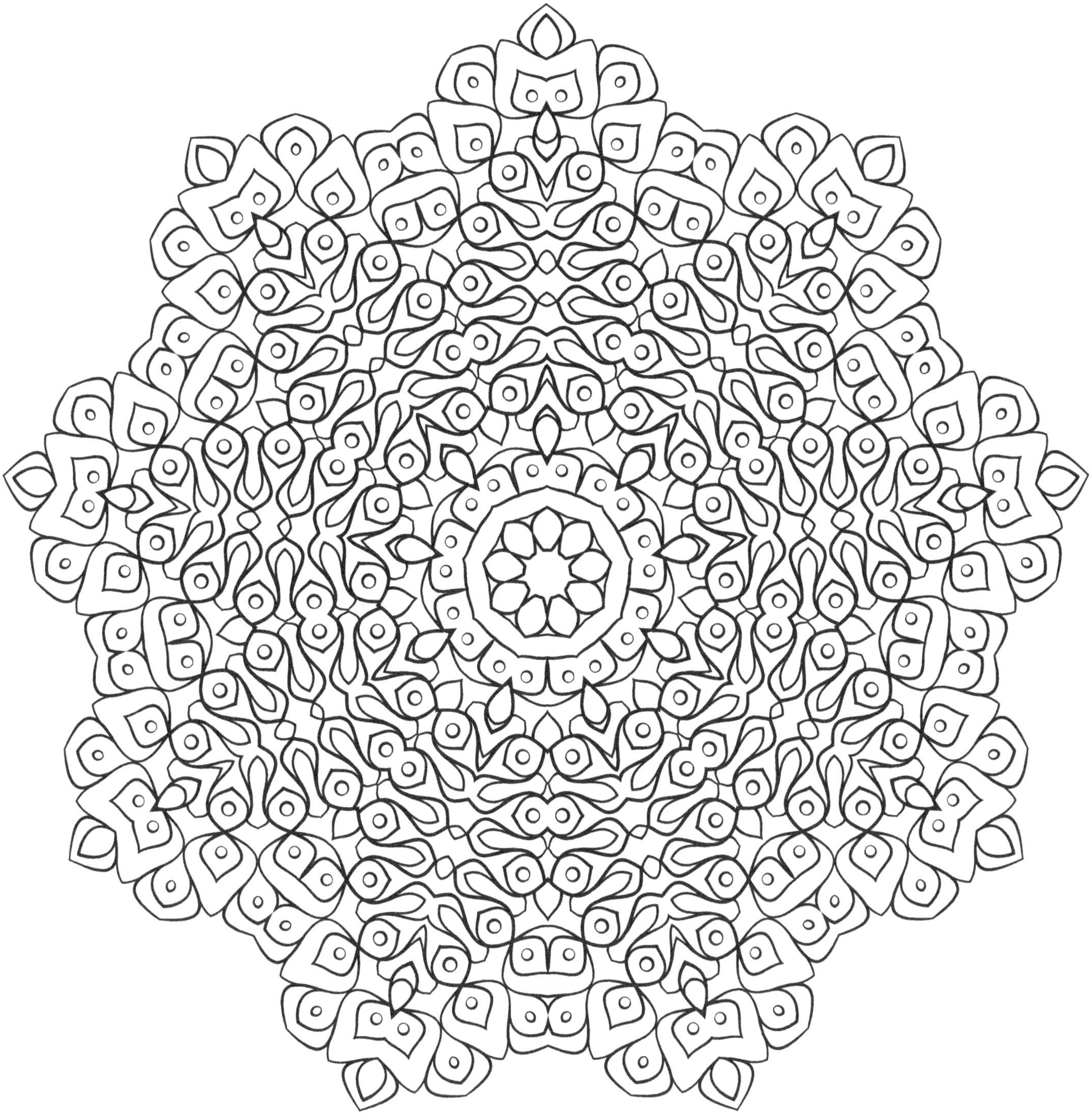

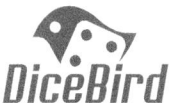

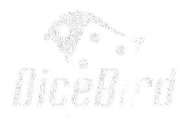

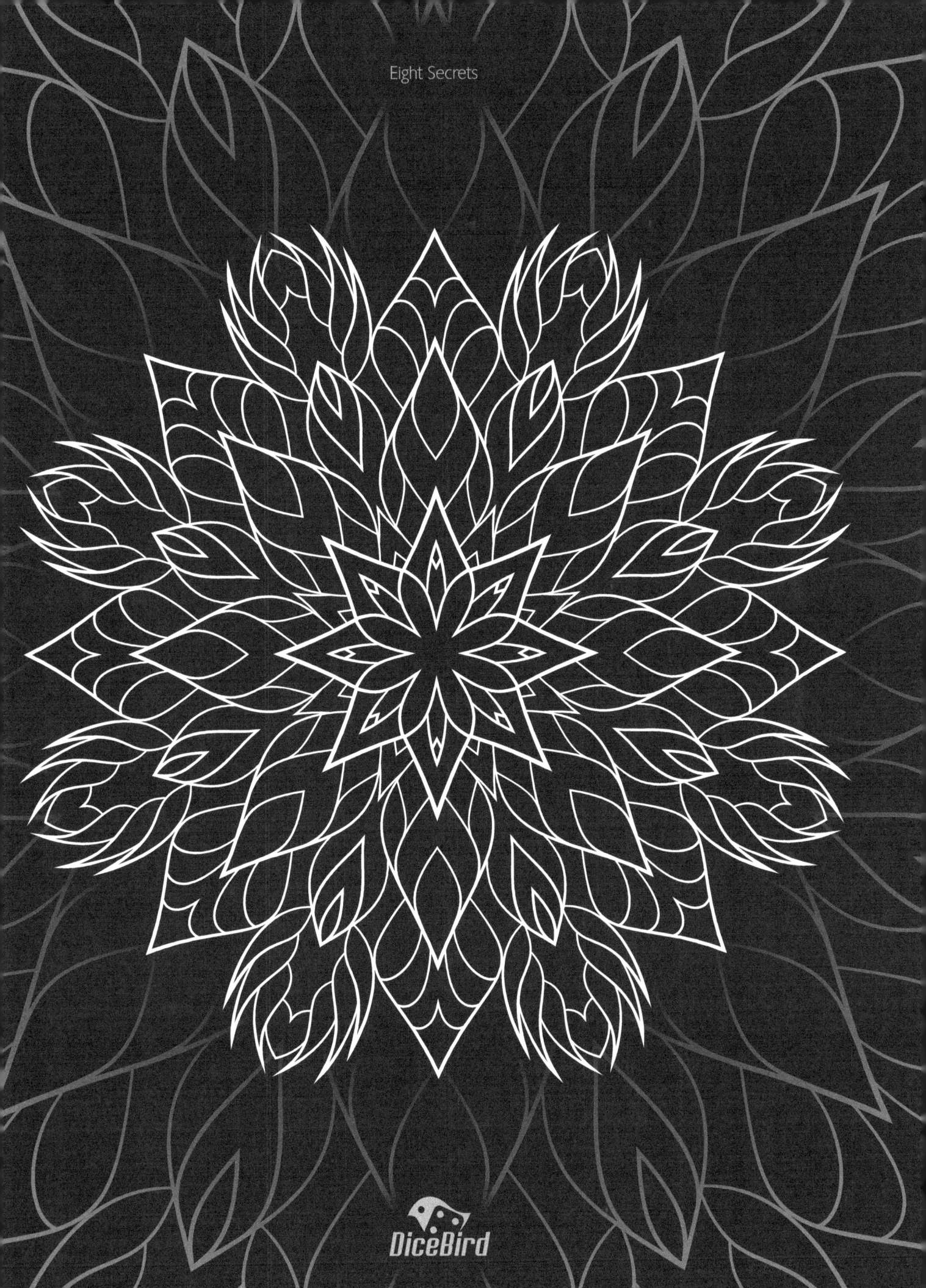

Eight Secrets

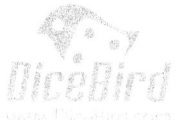

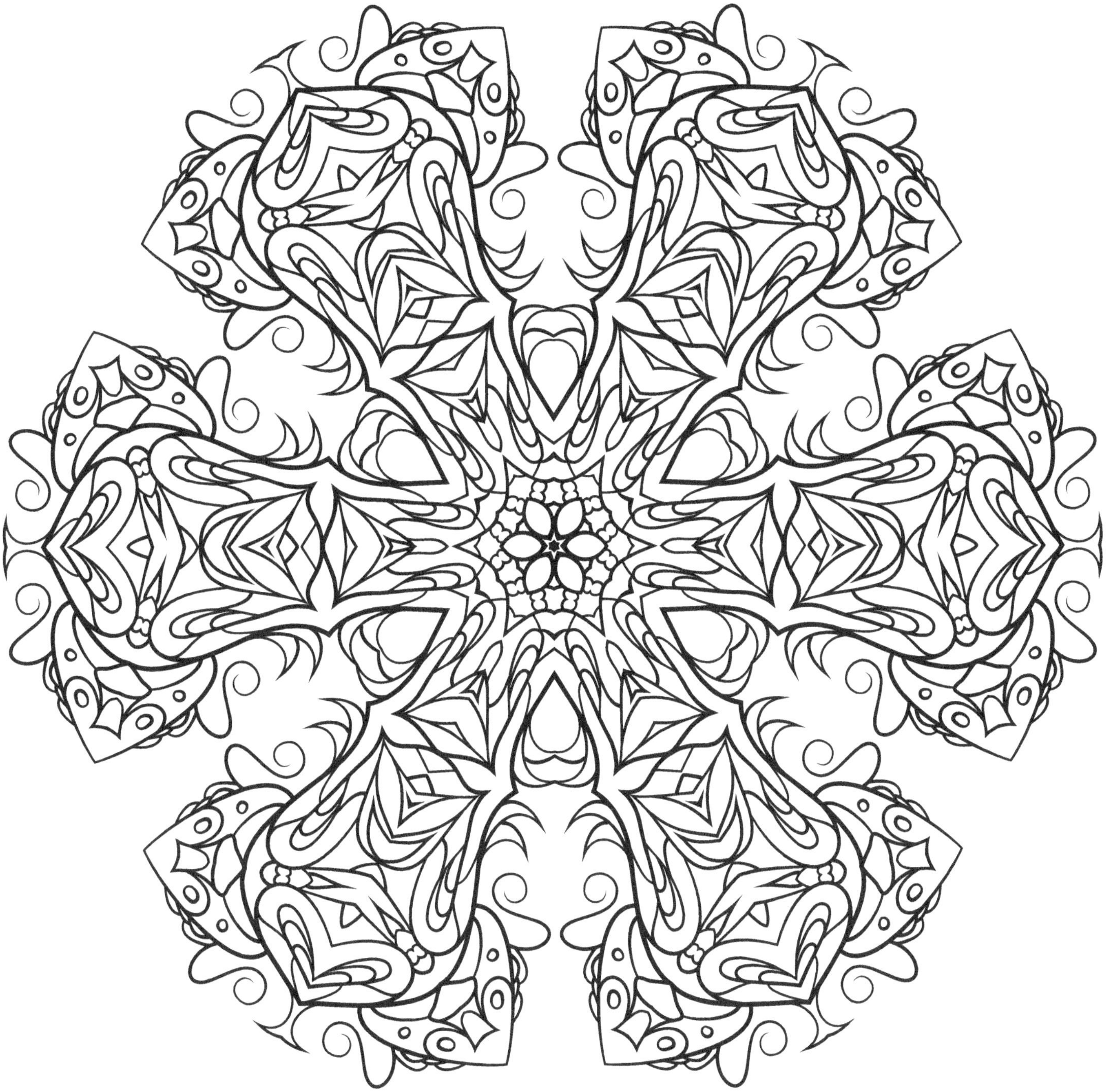

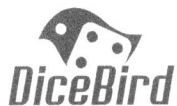

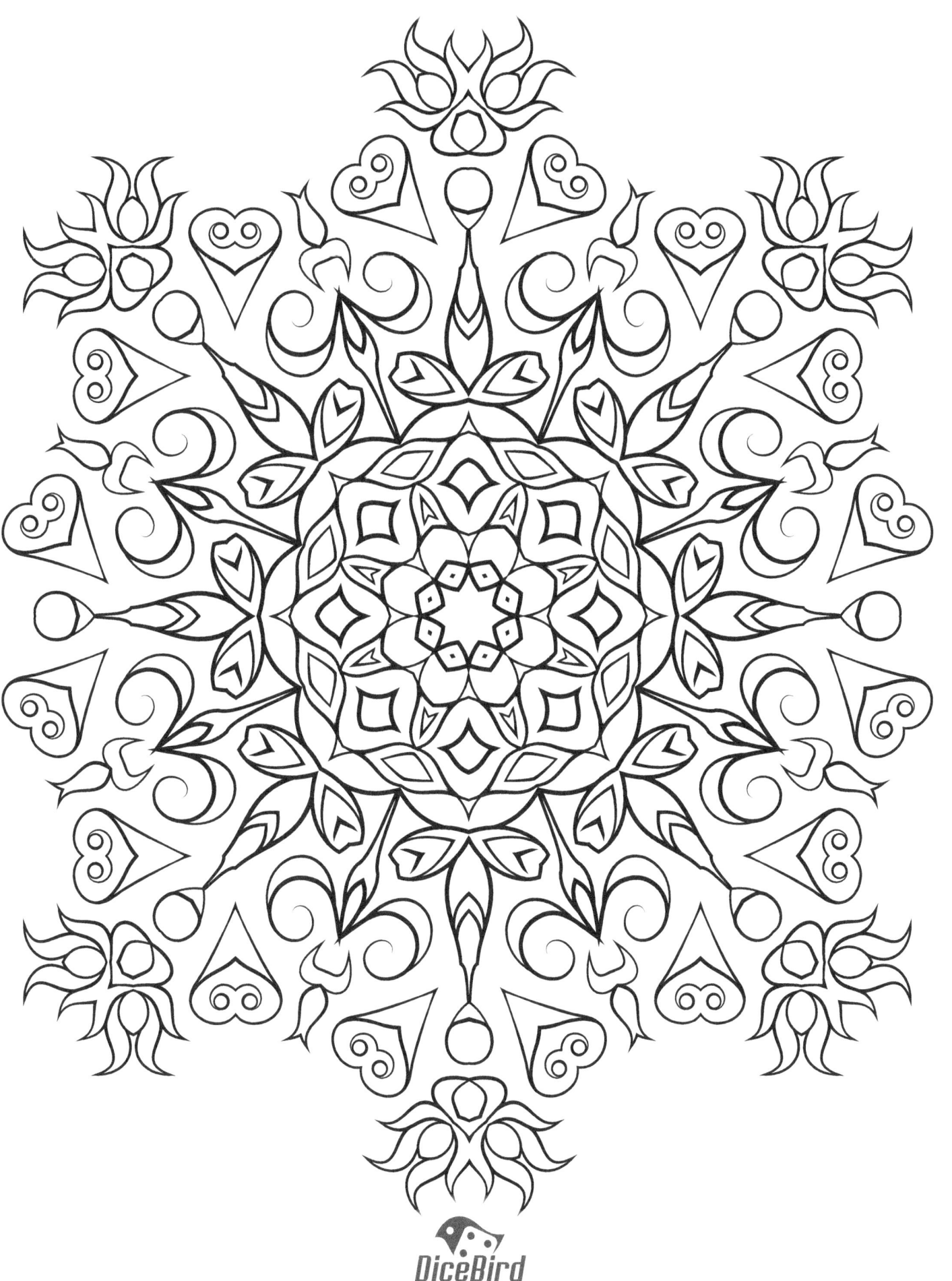

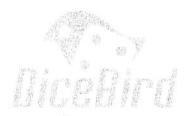

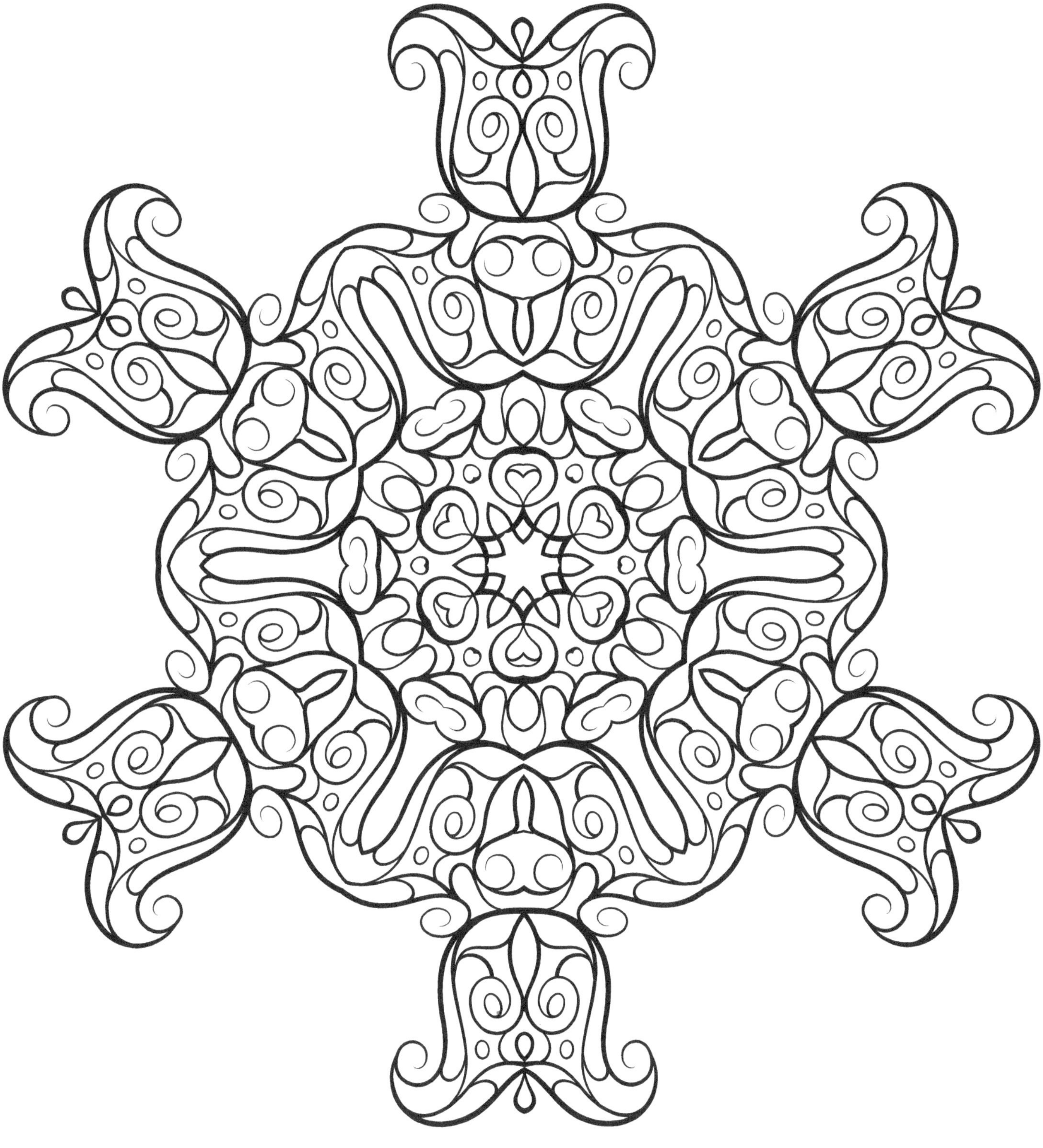

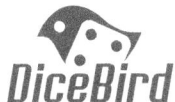

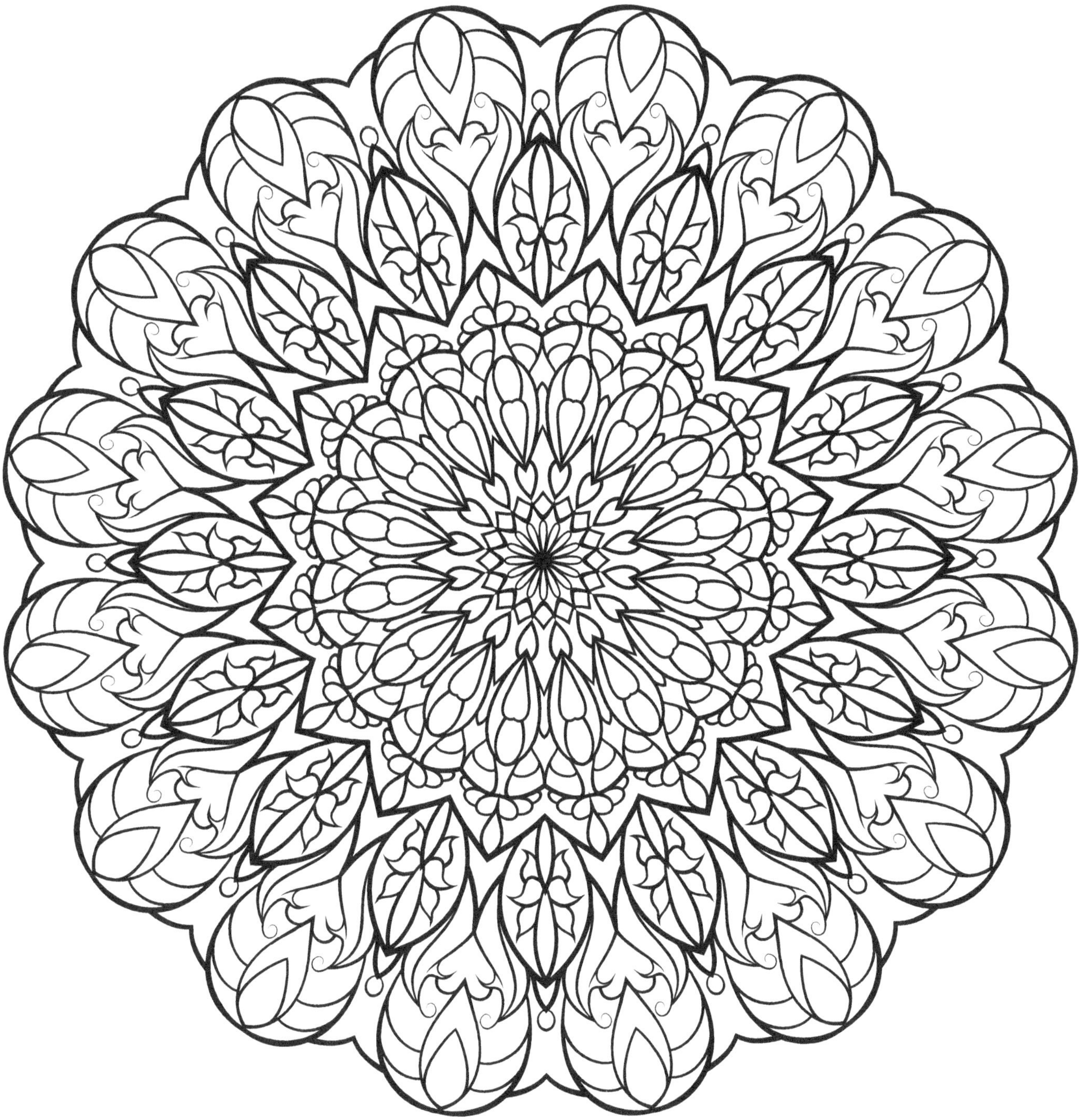

Mandala

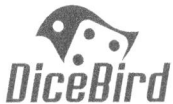

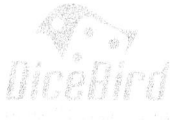

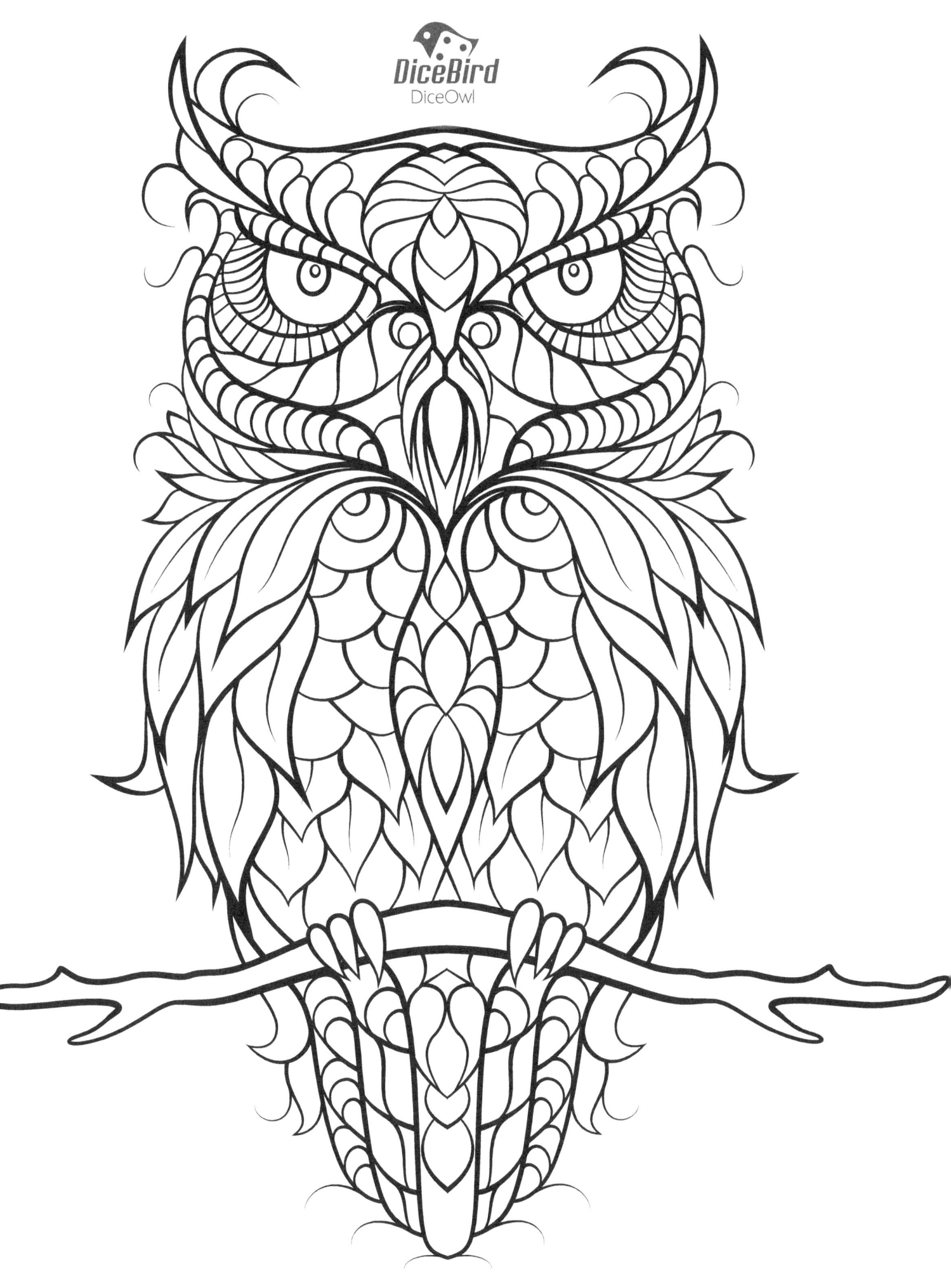

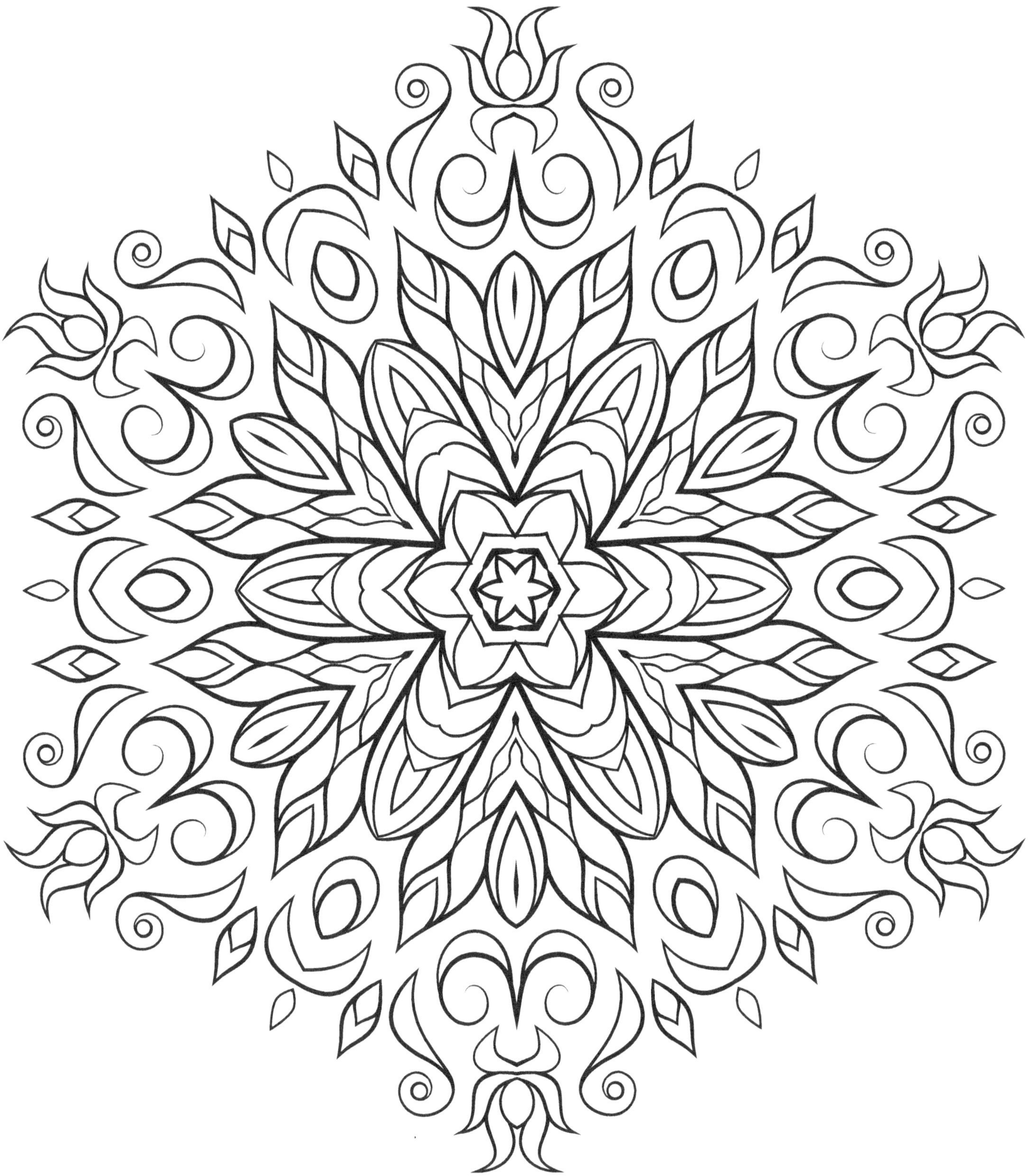

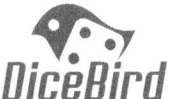

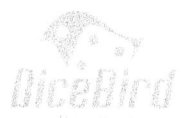

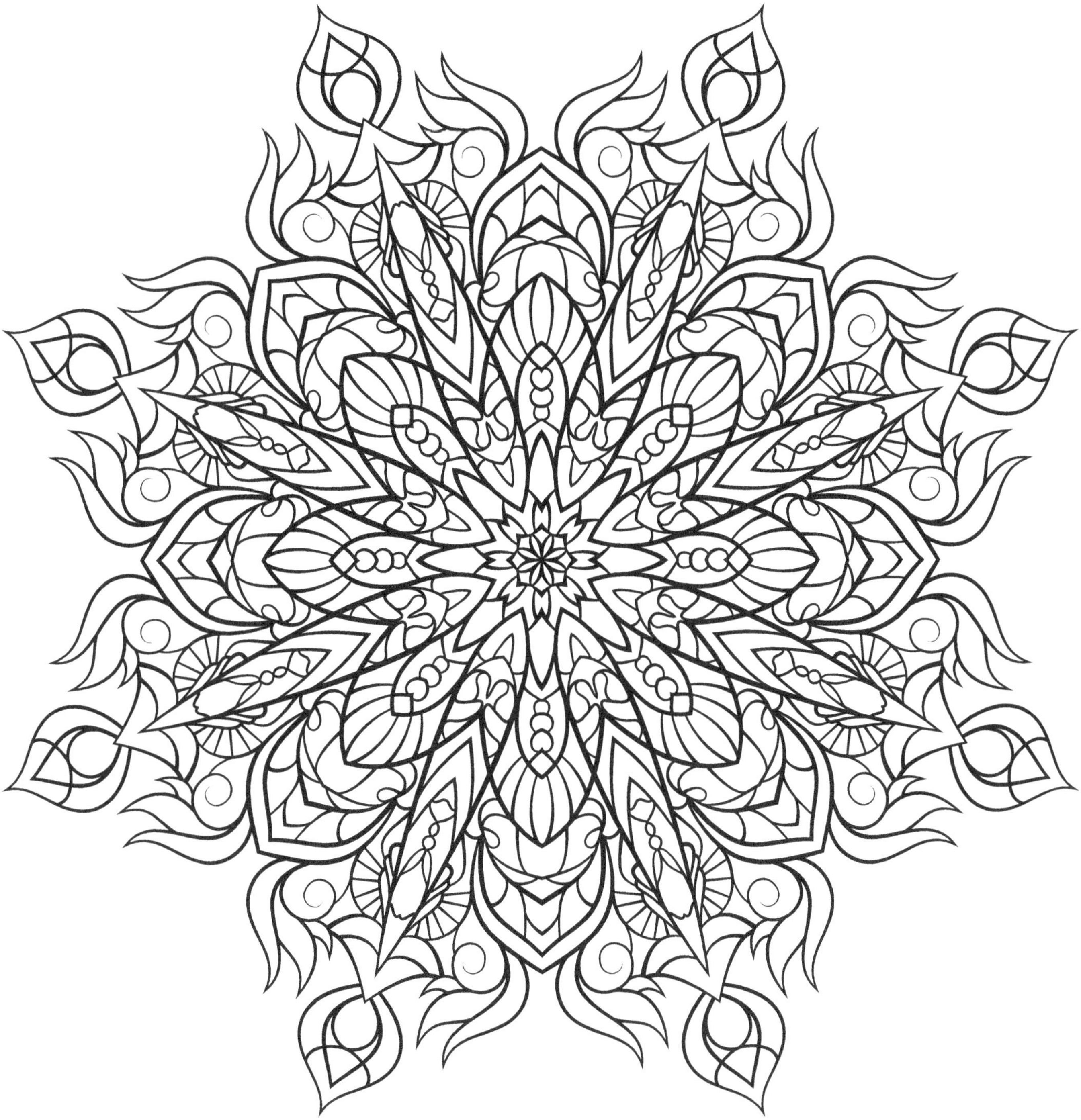

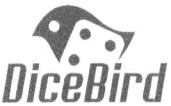

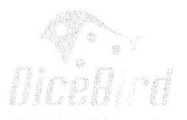

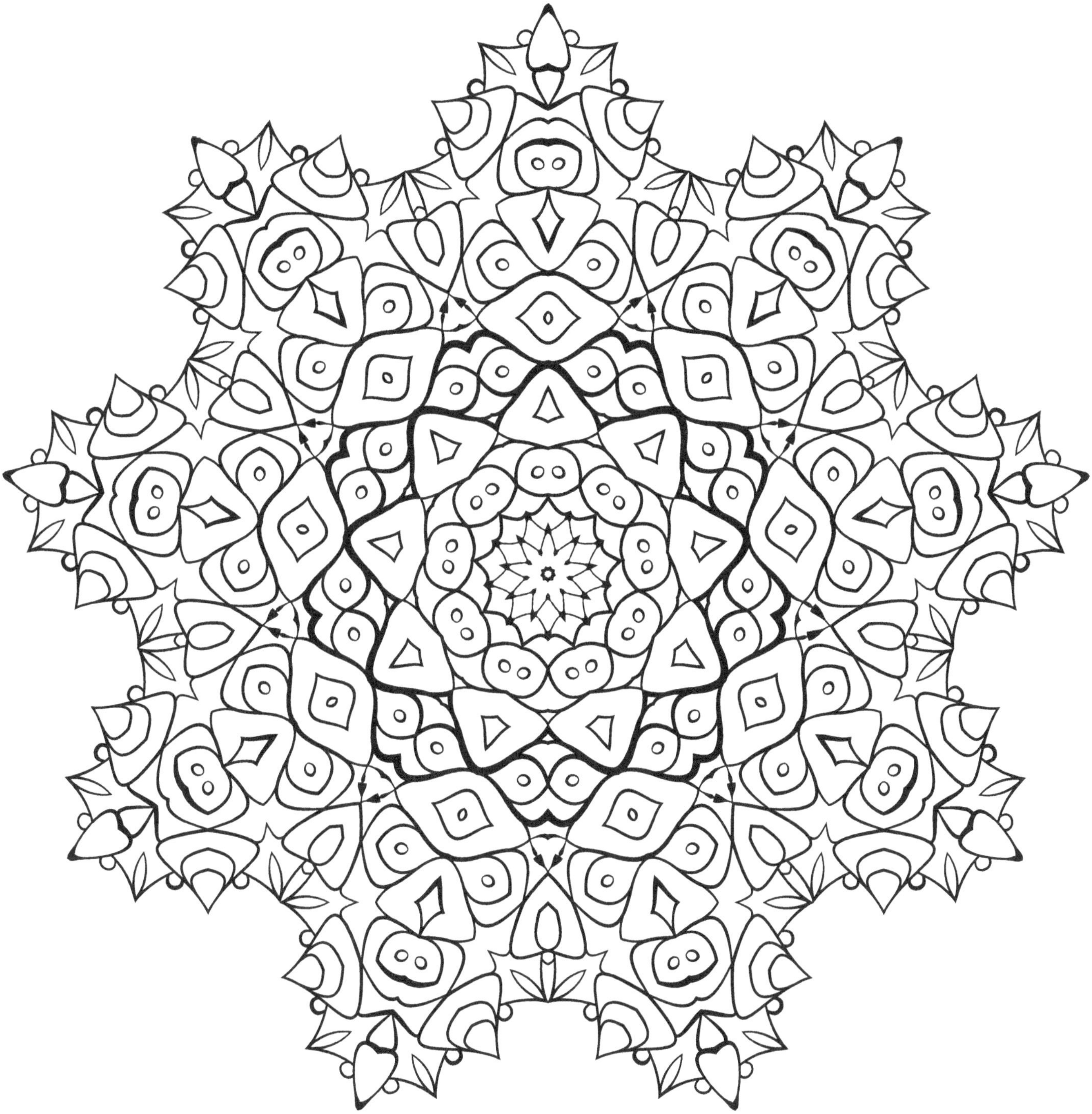

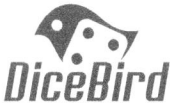

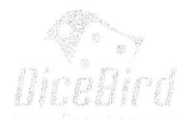

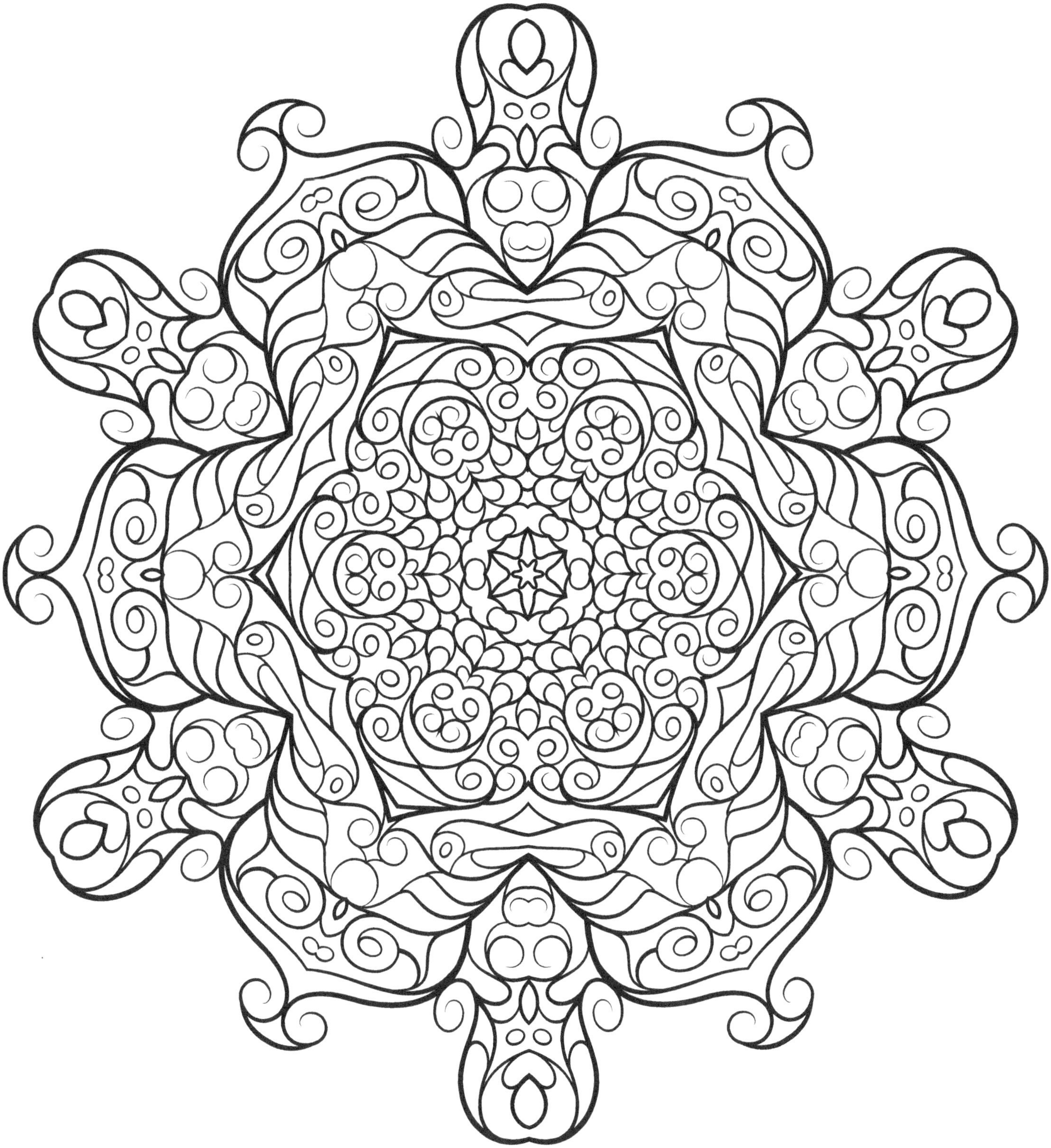

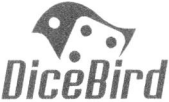

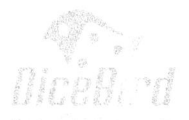

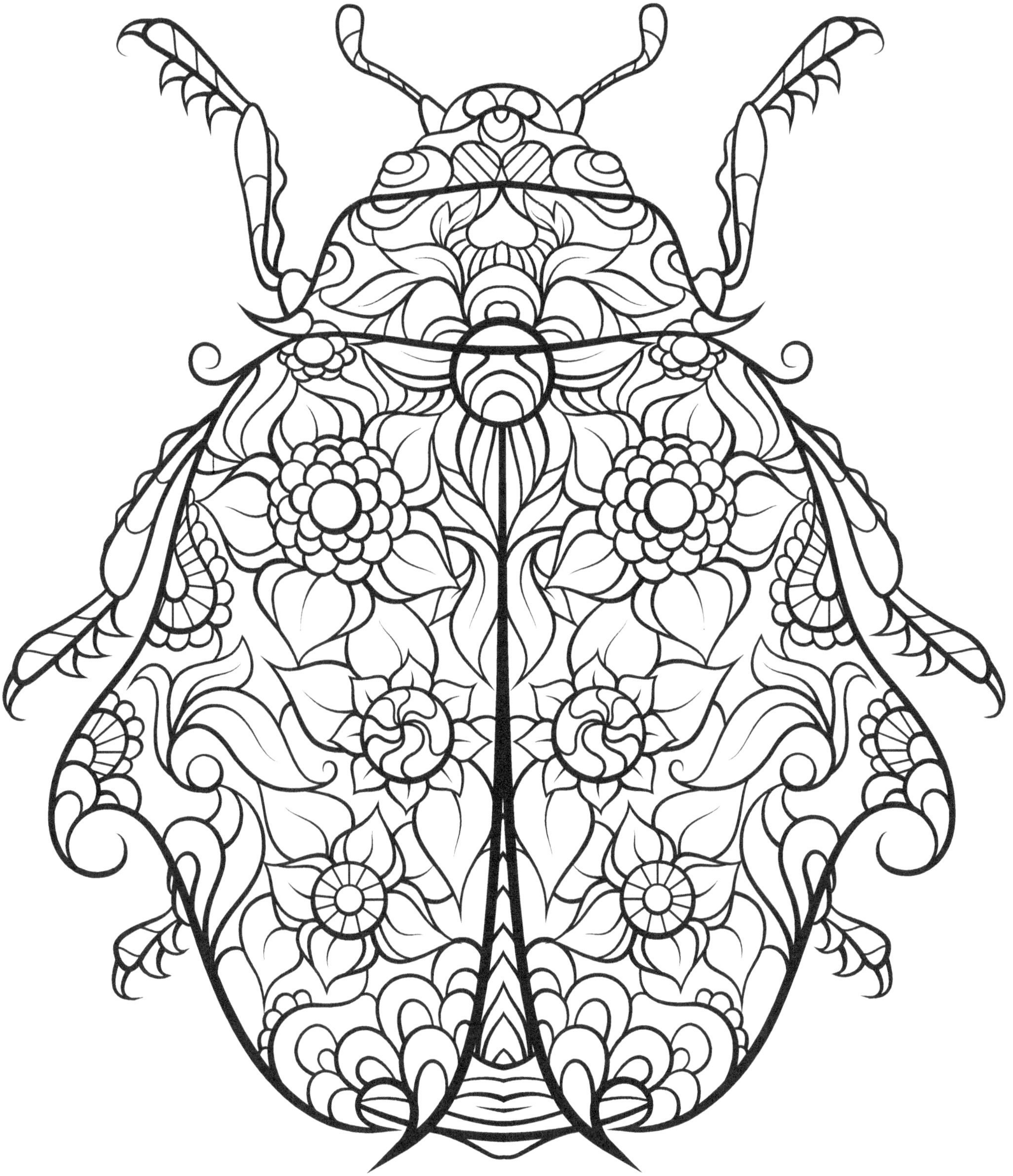

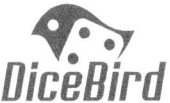

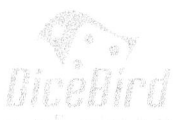

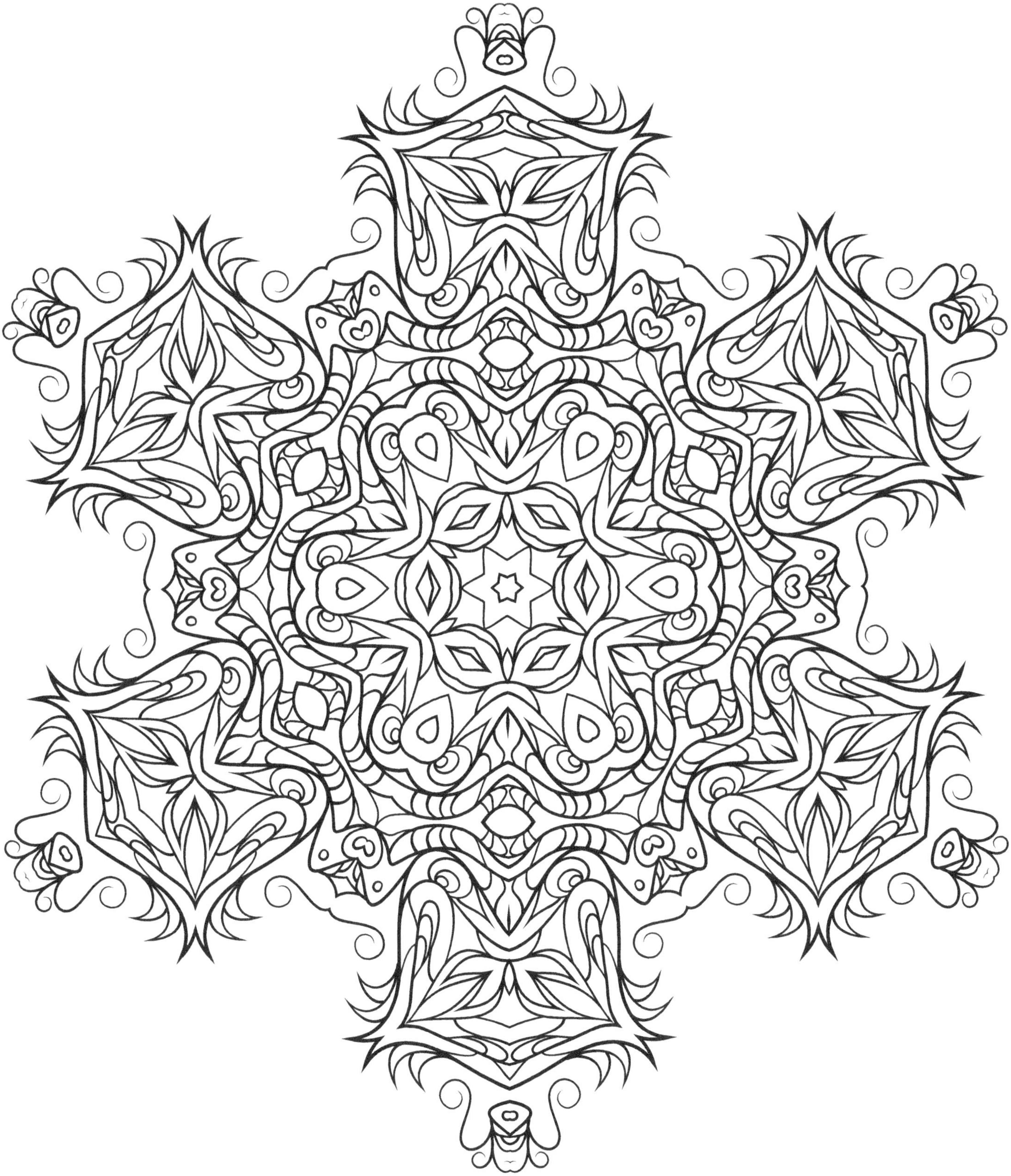

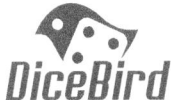

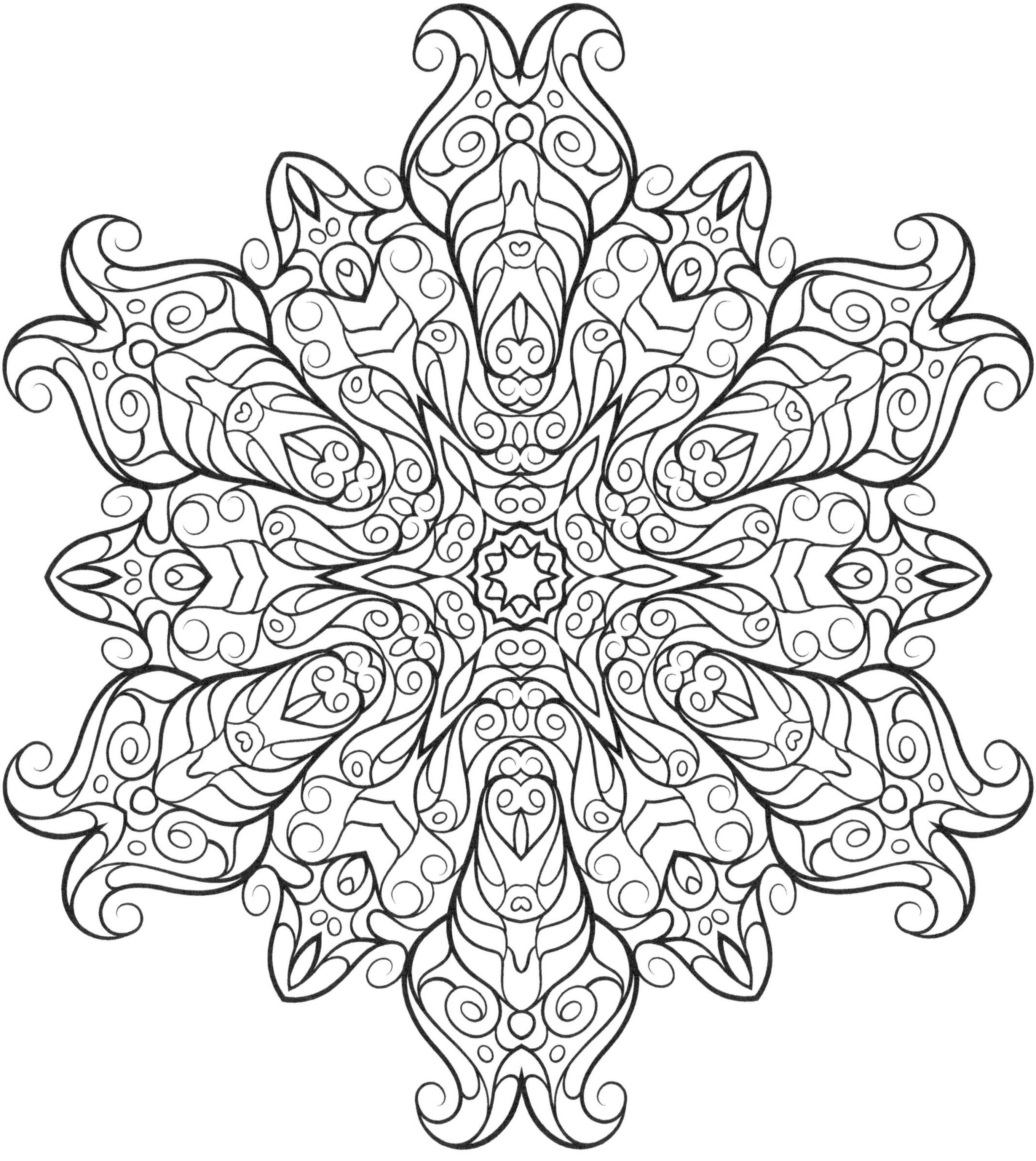

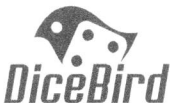

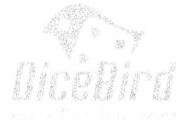

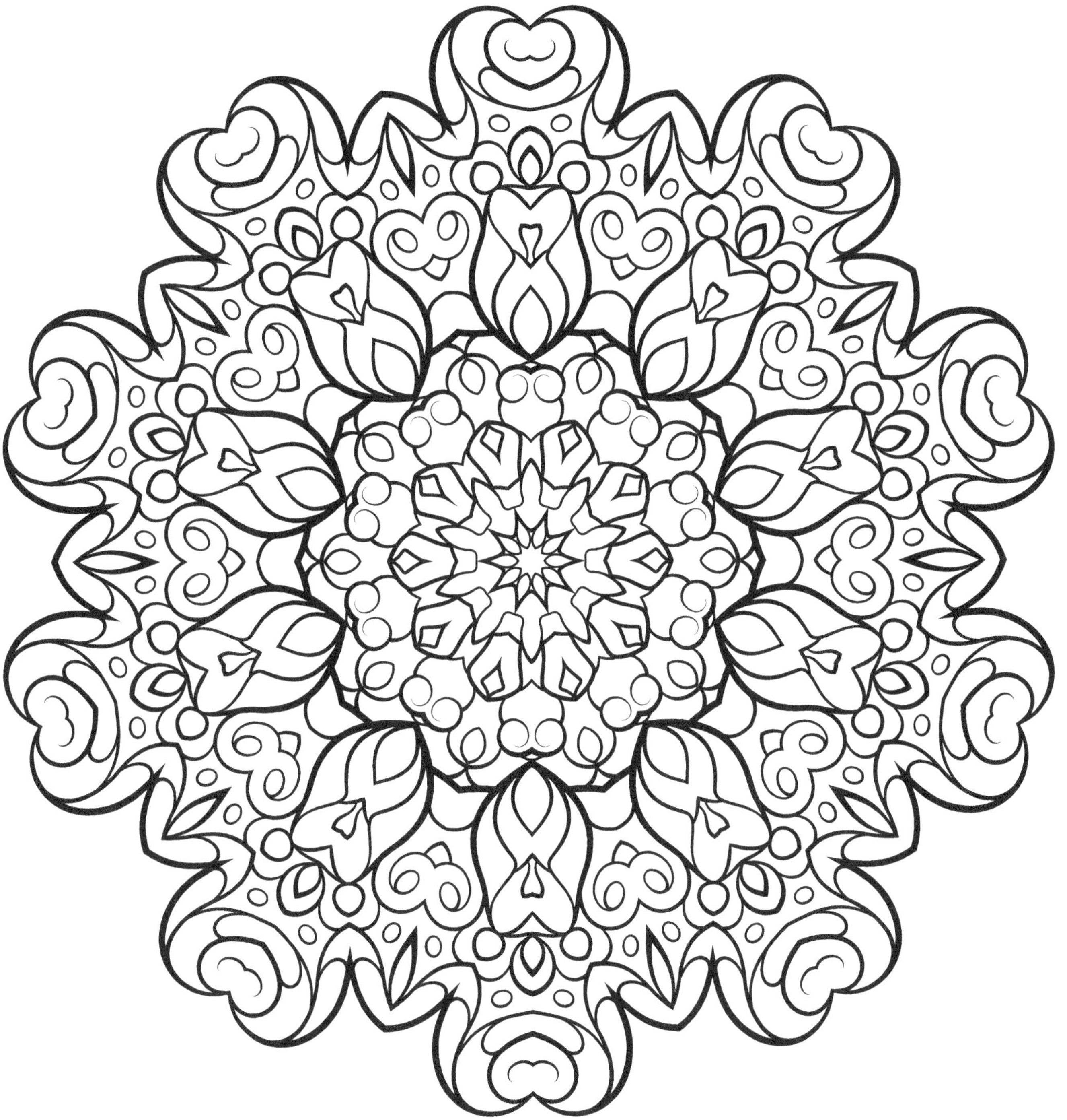

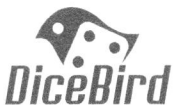

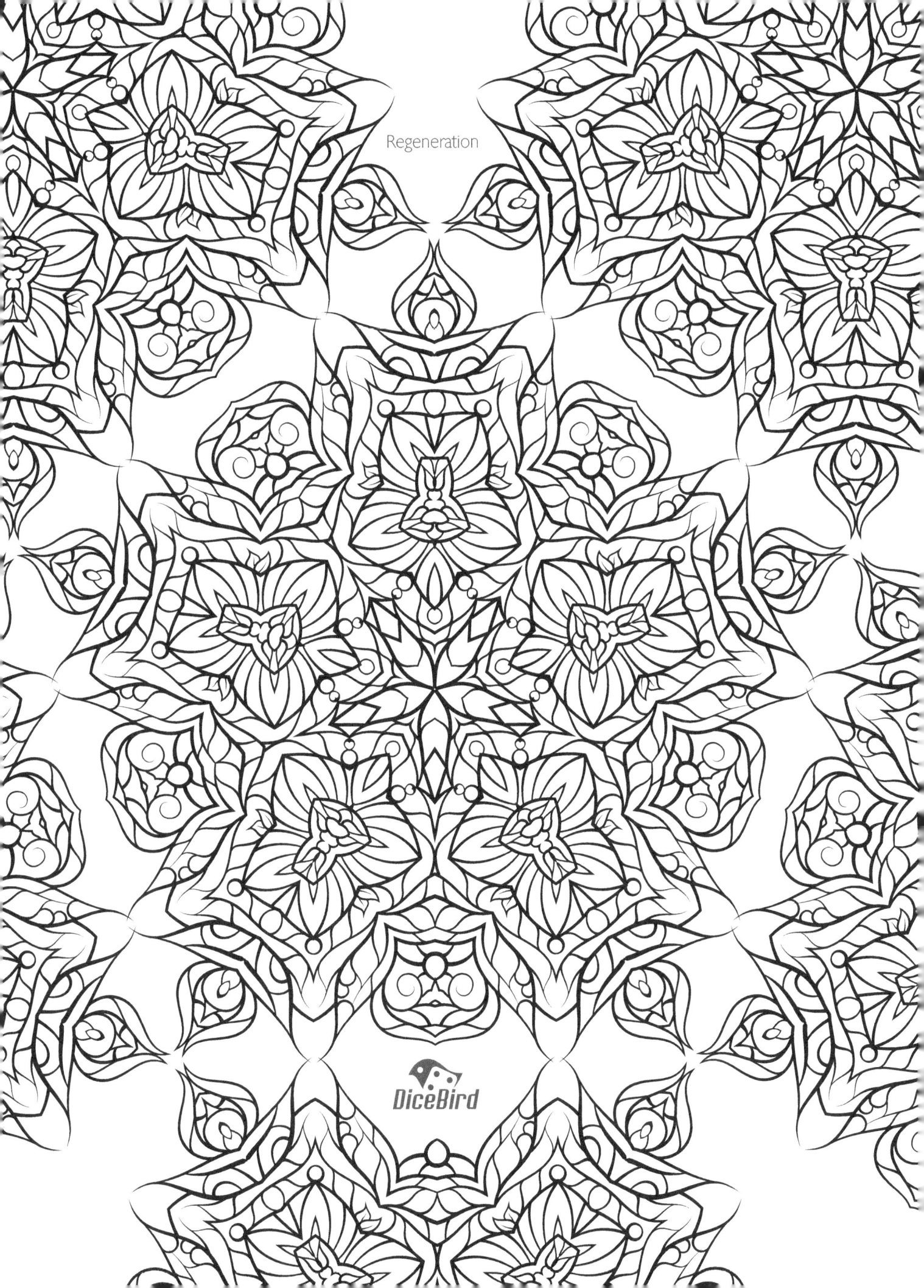

Regeneration

DiceBird

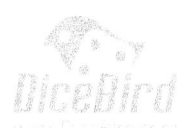

Arlene

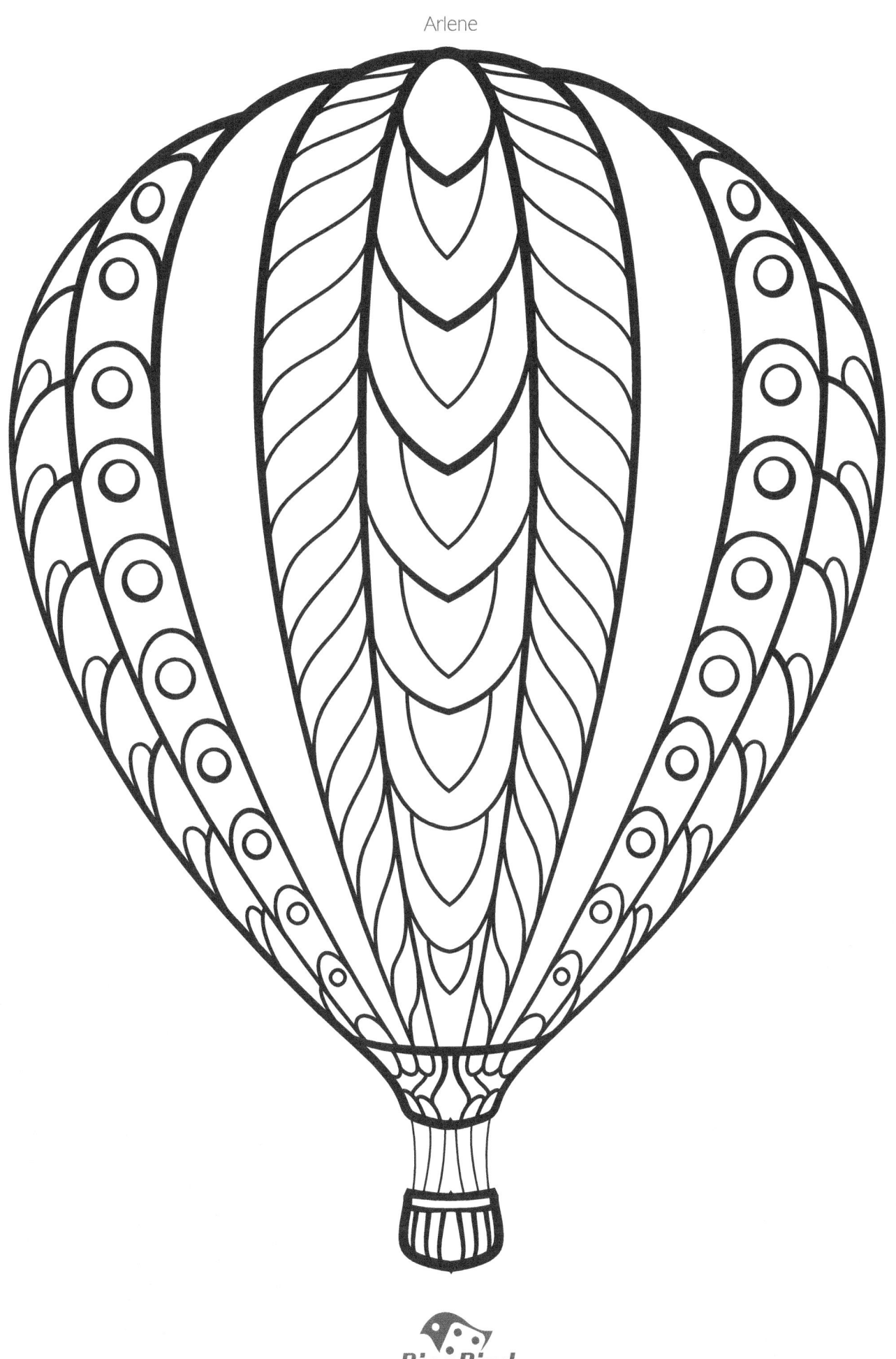

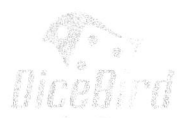

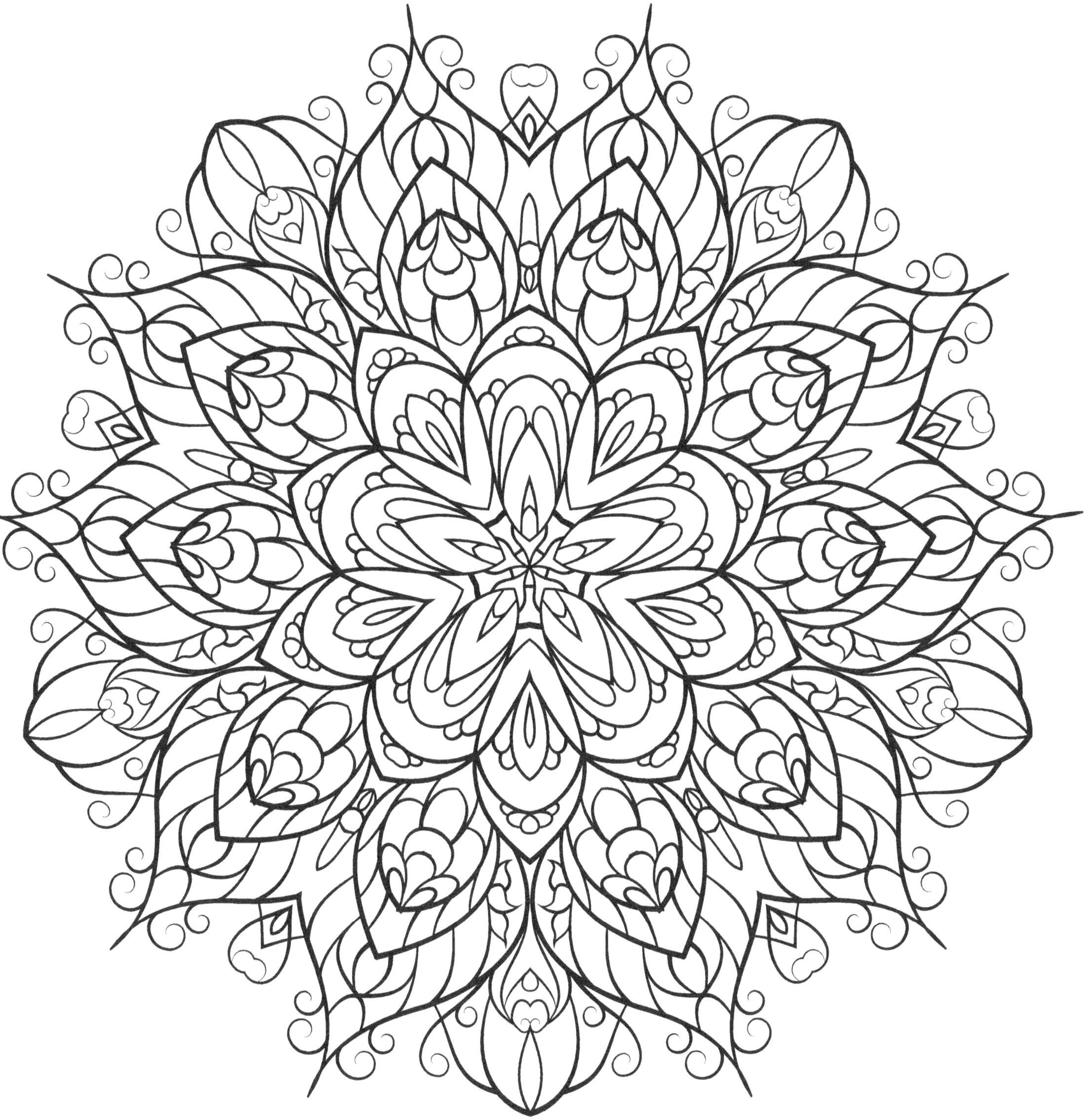

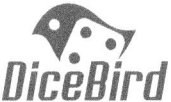

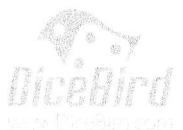

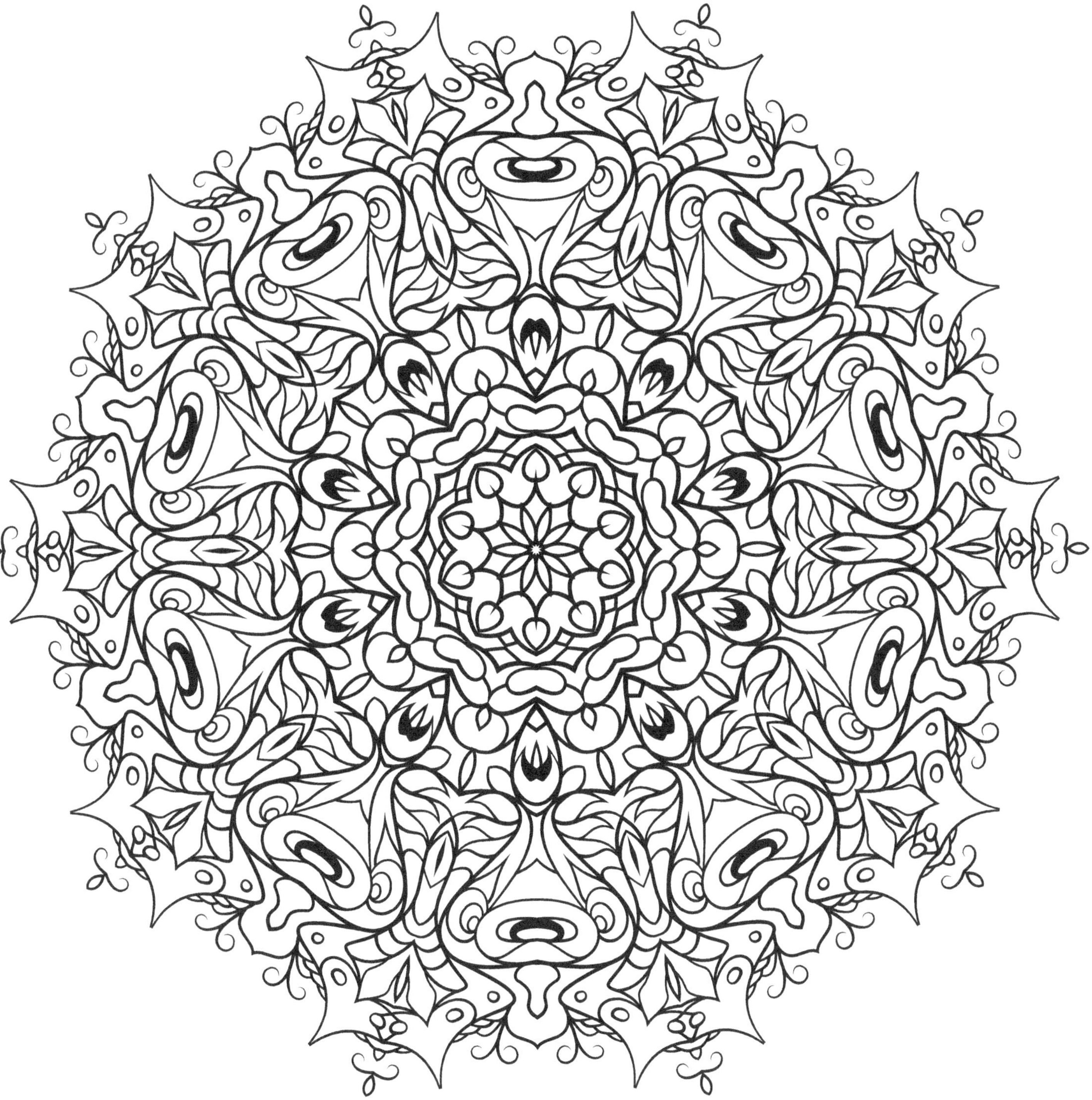

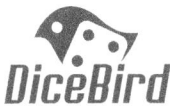

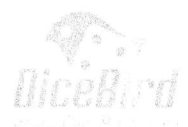

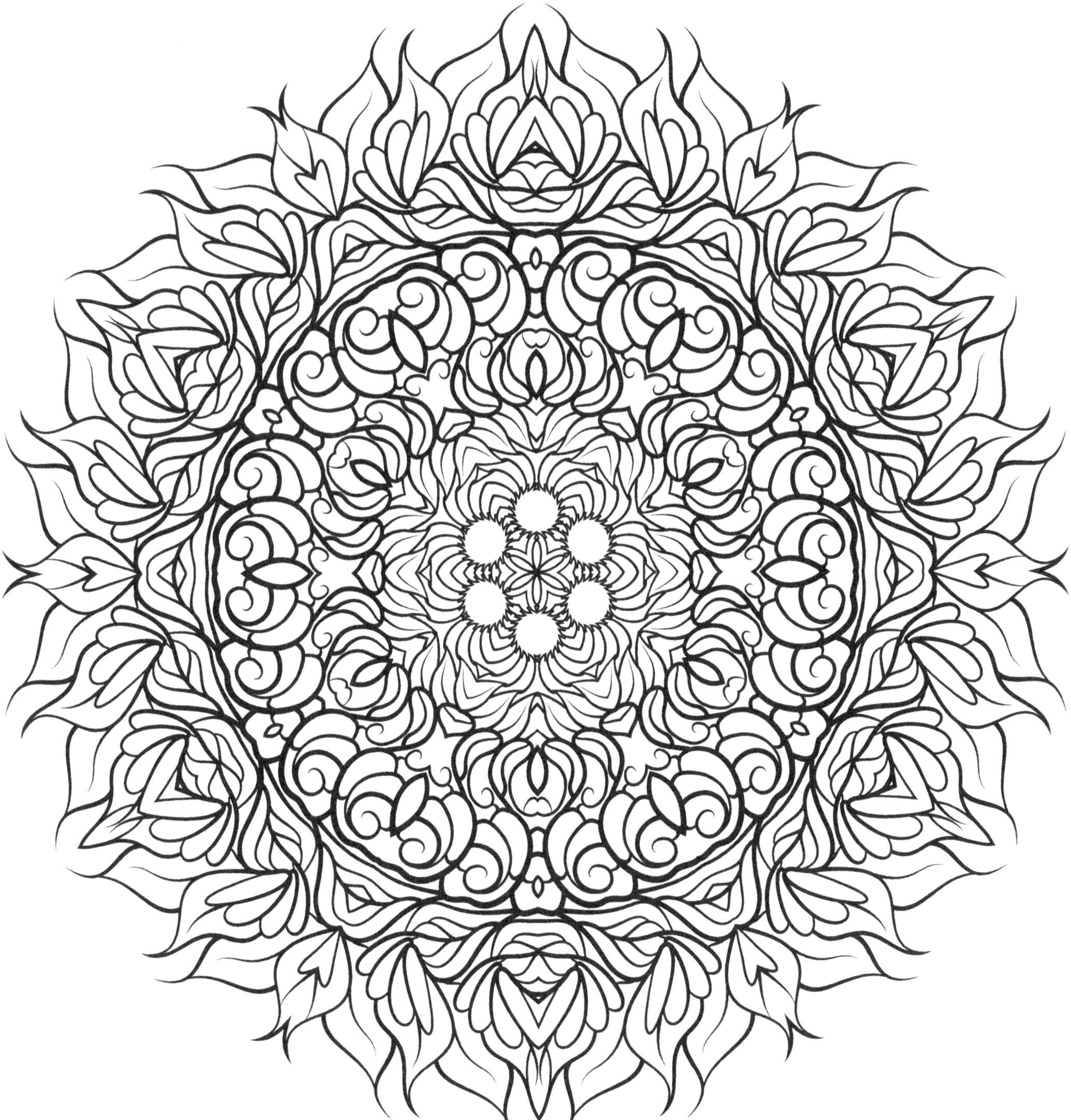

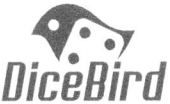

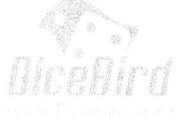

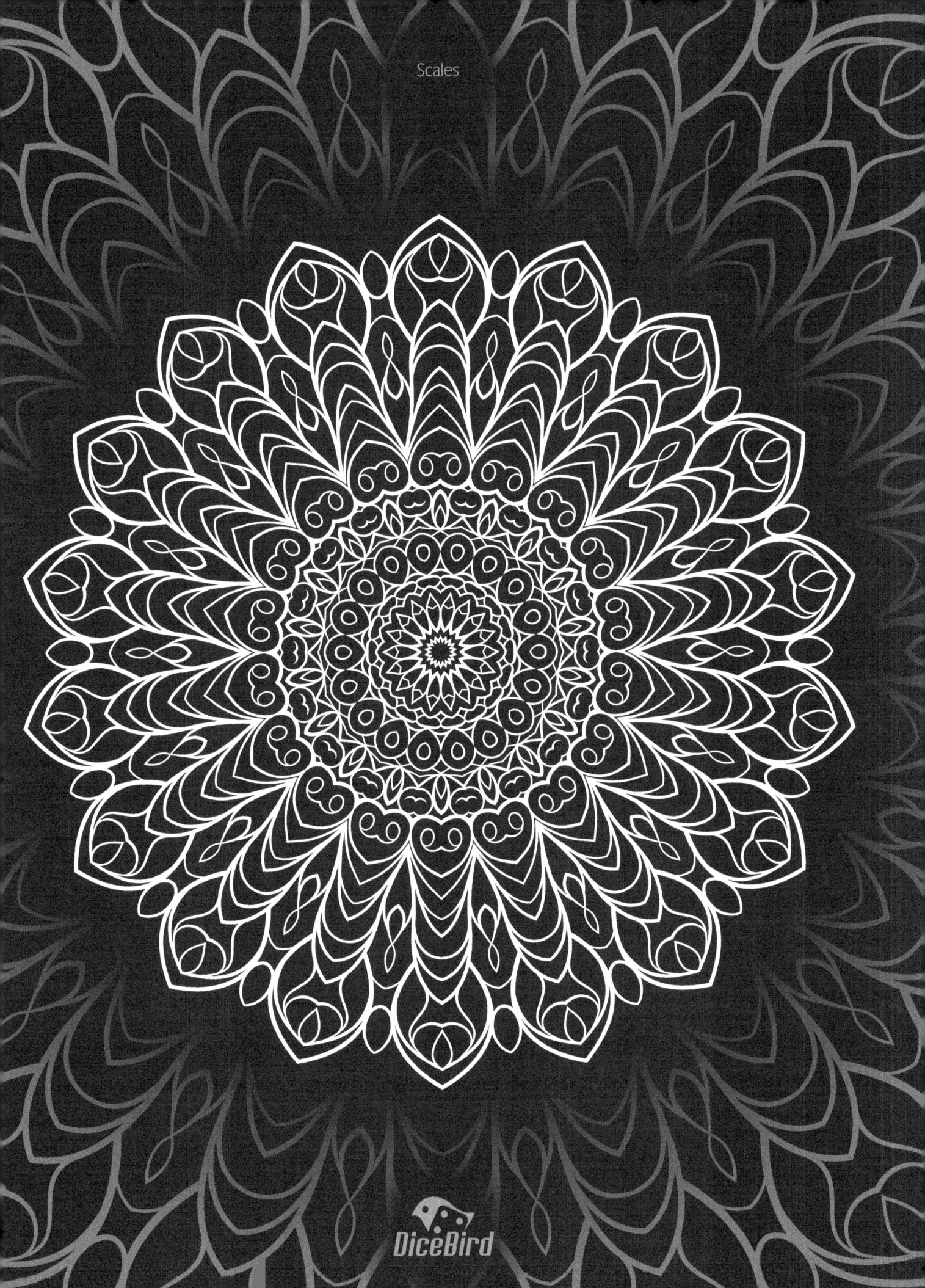

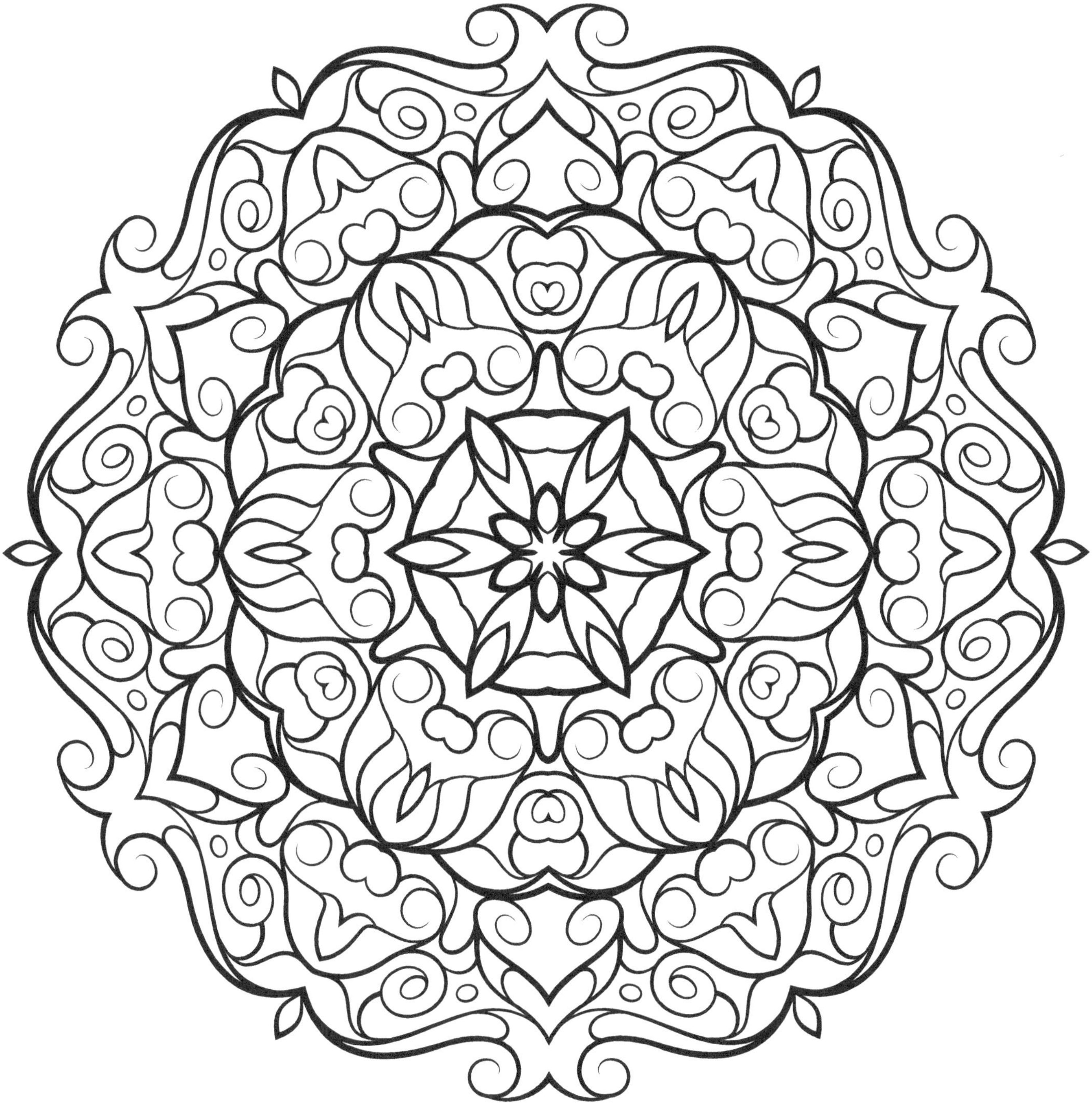

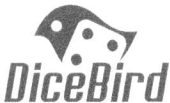

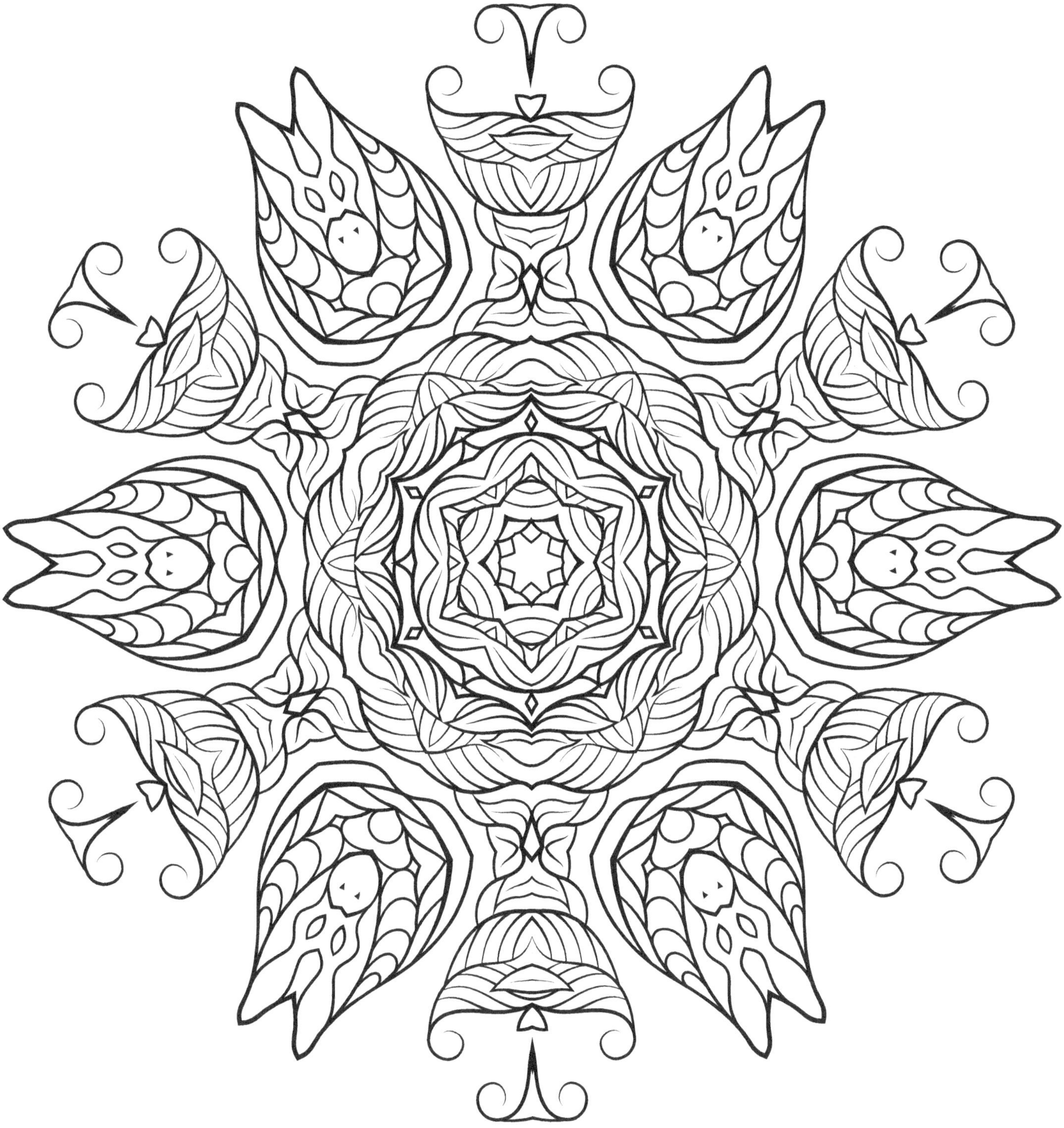

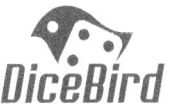

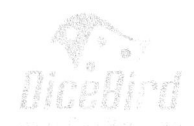

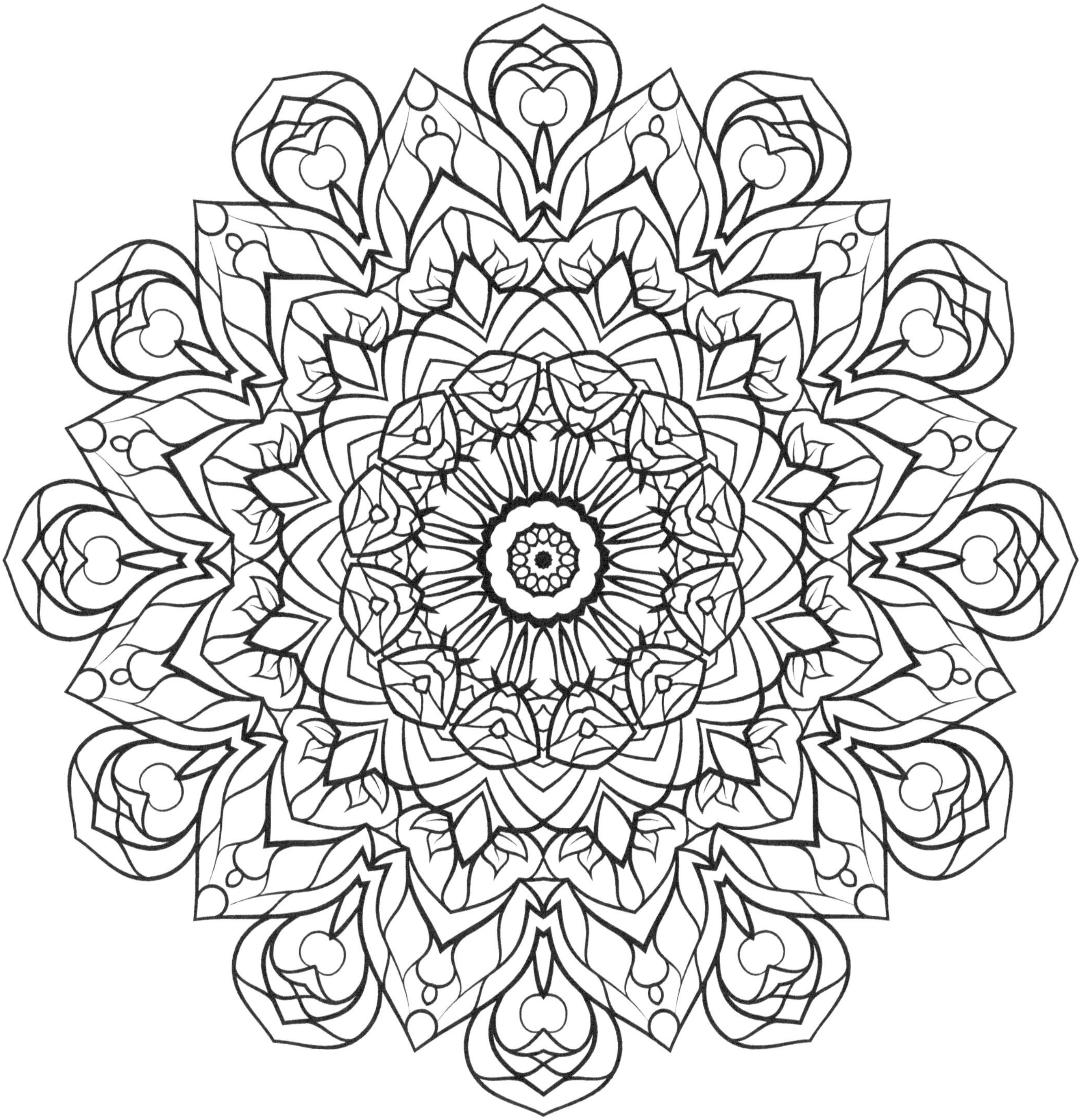

Camellias

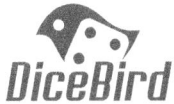

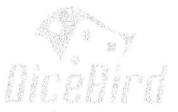

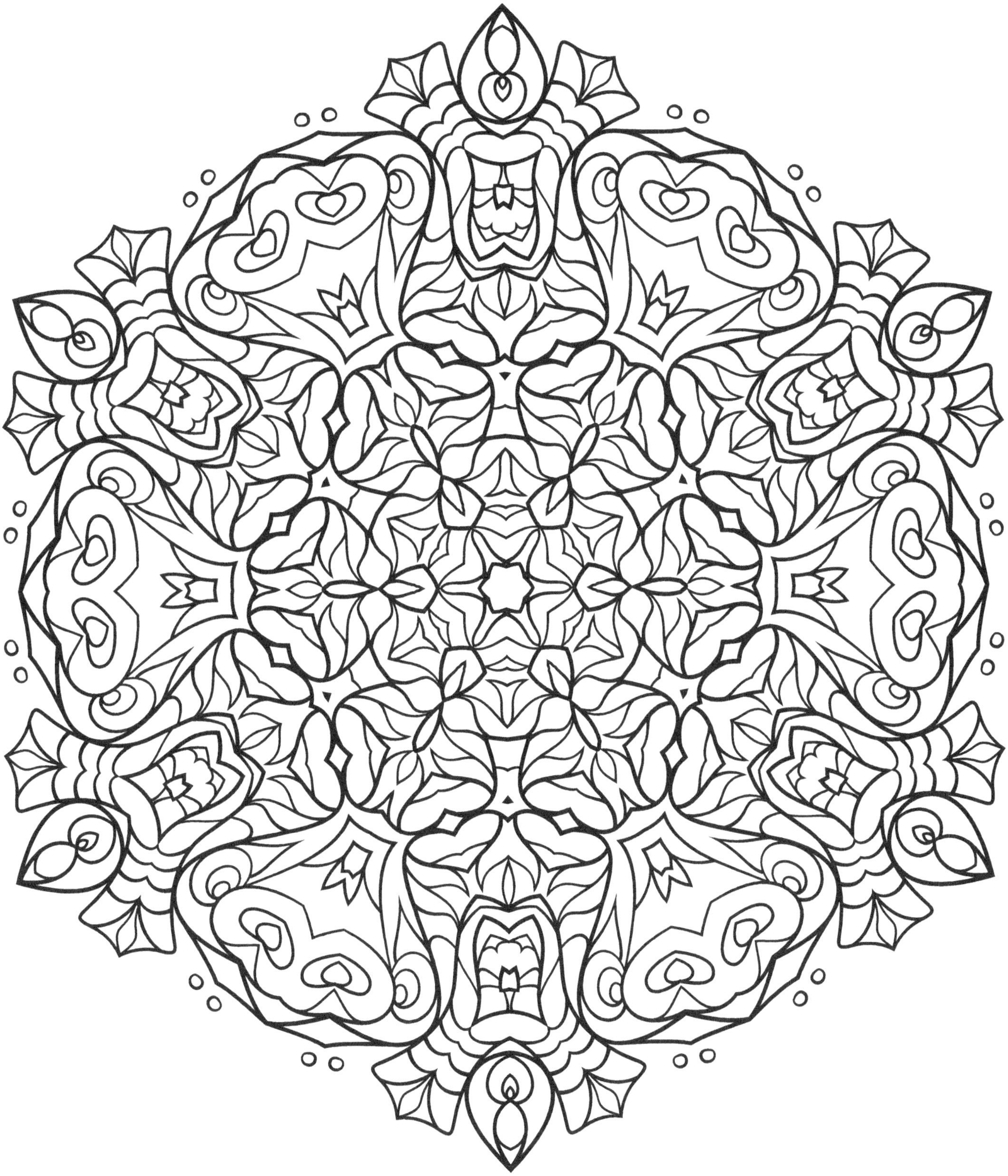

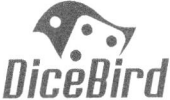

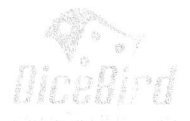

www.ingramcontent.com/pod-product-compliance
Lightning Source LLC
Chambersburg PA
CBHW080646180526
45168CB00008B/3327